® teach
yourself

how to win at poker
belinda levez

03001261000
op 5 .top1

For over 60 years, more than
40 million people have learnt over
750 subjects the **teach yourself**
way, with impressive results.

be where you want to be
with **teach yourself**

For UK order enquiries: please contact Bookpoint Ltd, 130 Milton Park, Abingdon, Oxon OX14 4SB. Telephone: +44 (0) 1235 827720. Fax: +44 (0) 1235 400454. Lines are open 09.00–17.00, Monday to Saturday, with a 24-hour message answering service. Details about our titles and how to order are available at www.teachyourself.co.uk

For USA order enquiries: please contact McGraw-Hill Customer Services, PO Box 545, Blacklick, OH 43004-0545, USA. Telephone: 1-800-722-4726. Fax: 1-614-755-5645.

For Canada order enquiries: please contact McGraw-Hill Ryerson Ltd, 300 Water St, Whitby, Ontario L1N 9B6, Canada. Telephone: 905 430 5000. Fax: 905 430 5020.

Long renowned as the authoritative source for self-guided learning – with more than 40 million copies sold worldwide – the **teach yourself** series includes over 300 titles in the fields of languages, crafts, hobbies, business, computing and education.

British Library Cataloguing in Publication Data: a catalogue record for this title is available from the British Library.

Library of Congress Catalog Card Number: on file.

First published in UK 2006 by Hodder Education, 338 Euston Road, London, NW1 3BH.

First published in US 2006 by Contemporary Books, a Division of the McGraw-Hill Companies, 1 Prudential Plaza, 130 East Randolph Street, Chicago, IL 60601 USA.

This edition published 2006.

The **teach yourself** name is a registered trade mark of Hodder Headline.

Typeset by Transet Limited, Coventry, England.
Printed in Great Britain for Hodder Education, a division of Hodder Headline, 338 Euston Road, London, NW1 3BH, by Cox & Wyman Ltd, Reading, Berkshire.

Hodder Headline's policy is to use papers that are natural, renewable and recyclable products and made from wood grown in sustainable forests. The logging and manufacturing processes are expected to conform to the environmental regulations of the country of origin.

Impression number   10 9 8 7 6 5 4 3 2 1
Year   2010 2009 2008 2007 2006

iii

contents

introduction		ix
01	**what is poker ?**	**1**
	origins of poker	2
	spread of poker	3
	poker today	6
	famous poker players	6
02	**playing tips**	**8**
	taking a sensible approach	9
	exchanging money for chips	9
	what does it cost to play?	10
	additional costs	11
	finding your game	12
	keep records	15
	appreciate your chances of winning	16
	vary your play	17
	know when to stop gambling	17
03	**the basic game**	**19**
	basics	20
	standard ranking of hands	22
	low poker	24
	additional rankings	26
	ranking hands with wildcards	29
	ranking of suits	30
	cards speak	31
04	**understanding the odds**	**32**
	how the odds change with different games	34
	draw games	34
	stud games	37

Texas hold 'em odds 38
pot odds 39
effect of using wildcards 40
05 betting 42
betting terms 43
developing a betting strategy 45
bluffing 46
knowing when to fold 46
betting in casinos 47
private games 47
straddle method 48
no-limit Texas hold 'em betting 49
freeze out 50
running out of money 50
06 bluffing 52
what is bluffing? 53
semi-bluffing 53
when should you bluff? 53
how often should you bluff? 57
spotting when other players are bluffing 58
07 body language 59
what is a tell? 60
bluffing and lying 60
tells to look for 61
controlling your body language 63
assessing the competition 64
type of player 65
online poker 65
08 cheating 66
holding cards 67
reflective surfaces 67
betting light 68
marked cards 68
technicians 69
cutting the cards 70

	stealing	71
	collusion	71
	cold deck	72
	false calling of a hand	72
	modern technology	72
	combatting cheating	72
	burning of cards	73
	shuffling and dealing the cards	74
09	**different games of poker**	**76**
	five-card draw	77
	five-card stud	78
	seven-card stud	80
	Texas hold 'em	82
	Omaha	85
	Caribbean stud poker	86
	pai gow poker	88
	three-card poker/progressive poker	90
	high card	92
	let it ride	92
10	**playing strategies**	**93**
	five-card draw	94
	five-card stud	98
	seven-card stud	101
	Texas hold 'em	103
	Omaha	107
	Caribbean stud poker	108
	pai gow poker	109
	let it ride strategy	111
11	**playing in private games**	**112**
	private games	113
	the law	114
	deciding the rules	116
	table etiquette	117
	hosting a private game	119
	strategies for playing	120

12 **playing in a casino**   **121**
       casinos   122
       selecting a casino   123
       playing in a casino   123
       how casino games vary from private games   124
       why gamble in a casino?   124
       costs   125
       entry requirements   126
       subliminal practices   126
       stakes   126
       how play is organized   127
       card room etiquette   127
       fairness of the game   128
       comps   130

13 **playing on the internet**   **131**
       what is internet poker?   132
       the history of internet poker   132
       is internet poker legal?   133
       why play internet poker?   134
       how fair is internet poker?   134
       cheating   134
       how internet poker works   135
       chatting to other players   139
       playing safe   139
       phishing   141
       all-in abuse   141
       disputes with internet poker sites   141
       playing strategy   142

14 **tournament play**   **143**
       poker tournaments   144
       types of tournament   145
       costs   146
       entry requirements   146
       how play is organized   147
       prizes   147

	satellites	148
	UK competitions	148
	internet tournaments	149
	speed tournaments	150
	major tournaments	150
	playing tips	152
15	**poker dice**	**155**
	how to play	156
	playing the game	158
	keeping score	160
	number of cards used	161
16	**video poker machines**	**162**
	what is video poker?	163
	types of machine	163
	how to play	163
	payout odds for different games	164
	playing tips	166
	basic strategy for jacks or better	167
	deuces wild strategy	168
	kings or better joker wild strategy	168
glossary		**170**
taking it further		**174**
index		**177**

introduction

Poker is a game that is easy to learn and fun to play. Most people learn to play poker at home with family and friends. The stakes are often low, just piles of matchsticks and your pride. However, playing for money, especially with strangers, is an entirely different experience.

You may have found yourself in the following situation: You are at a party/gathering and get chatting to a stranger. 'Can you play poker?' he asks. The question seems innocent enough and he appears friendly, so you answer 'Yes' and find yourself invited to play a game. You are introduced to the stranger's friends who warmly welcome you. You feel relaxed and confident, especially after you've won the first couple of pots, but then your luck changes. A few hours later your wallet is lighter and you are wiser. You have learnt that playing poker is easy but winning money at poker is not. You also no longer trust your new friends. You begin to wonder whether they were, perhaps, cheating. Some of the hands you were dealt were really good but your opponents always managed to have better hands. You have just had your first real poker lesson and it cost you a lot of money.

To play poker well takes skill, knowledge and lots of practice. This book aims to teach you how to win at poker. You will be shown the basic principles of the game and given advice on where to gamble and the associated costs involved. The dangers of playing in private games with strangers are also highlighted and you are shown how to spot cheats. You will be taught how to get better value for money and methods of play that maximize winnings while keeping losses to a minimum. Popular variations of the game are described and strategies given for each game, which you should adapt according to the strengths and weaknesses of your opponents.

There are many illustrated examples to make the understanding of the game easier. A glossary is included to define the jargon used in the book and some of the additional jargon that you may encounter.

By the end of this book you should be a more informed player with a better understanding of the game. With plenty of practice you should also become a more skilful player and, it is to be hoped, a winner instead of a loser.

Good luck

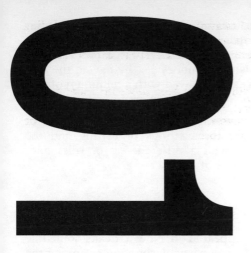

01

what is poker?

In this chapter you will learn:
- why people play poker
- about the history of poker
- about famous poker players.

Poker is the name given to a huge number of card games. What they have in common is that they are based on the ranking of five-card hands. The basic game is relatively easy to learn. The object of the game is to win the money bet by having the best ranking hand. The games can be played with a minimum of two players but around five to seven players is more practical.

The rules of individual games vary enormously. The number of cards dealt to each player, the methods of betting and the ranking of the hands all mean a different set of rules and, therefore, a very different type of game.

Origins of poker

The game of poker first appeared in New Orleans sometime during the 18th century. It was particularly popular among the French settlers. The origins of the game are not documented but it probably evolved from a combination of other card or dice games.

After the arrival of playing cards in Europe in the 14th century, new games were continually being invented and adapted. Rules were rarely written down. There are several European card games that have similarities to poker. These include the French game of poque, the German game of Pochen, the English game of brag and the Italian game of primero. None of these games is a direct descendant of poker but they have most likely had an influence on it. The term flush, for example, comes from primero, which dates from the 16th century. In primero, four cards of the same suit was called a *flux* leading to the term flush, which is used in poker to denote a hand of the same suit. The name for poker was probably derived from the French game poque.

One game that has the greatest similarity to poker is the Persian game of as nas, which dates from the 16th century. It was played with a deck of 25 cards with five suits. Each player would initially be dealt two cards. A round of betting would follow. A further two cards were dealt, followed by a round of betting. A fifth card would be dealt, followed by another round of betting. Hands were ranked in a similar way to poker. The highest ranking hand was five of the same suit (equivalent to a flush in poker) followed by five of a kind. A full house of three of a kind with a pair also features in the ranking. As well as betting, the game also allowed players to bluff.

It is also possible that poker was adapted from dice games. Poker is based on the ranking of hands. Dice games with the same principle, the ranking of throws, have been played for at least 2000 years. A Roman dice game called tali is based on the ranking of throws where three of a kind beats a pair, much like poker.

The first written account of poker comes from the diary of Joseph Crowell, an English actor, who was touring America in 1829. He described it as a game where players each received five cards and made bets. The highest combination of cards won.

In 1834, in his book *An Exposure of the Arts and Miseries of Gambling*, Jonathan H. Green, gave an account of what he called the 'cheating game'. He saw it being played while travelling on the Mississippi River on a steamboat which was heading for New Orleans. A deck of 20 cards was used with each player receiving a hand of five. The player with the highest ranking hand would win. The hands were ranked as pairs, three of a kind and four of kind. This early form of poker featured no draws. The players simply received five cards face down and would bet on the cards received.

The 20-card deck was replaced by a 32-card deck and, by 1833, a 52-card deck had been introduced. Brief mentions of poker were made in *Hoyles' Games* in 1850 where it was described as a game for 10 players where each player received five cards face down.

Spread of poker

New Orleans had numerous gambling establishments where poker was played including the Crescent City House, a luxury casino that was opened by John Davis in 1827. As America was settled, poker spread and was played on boats that travelled along the Mississippi and Ohio Rivers. Professional gamblers known as sharps made their living by playing cards with riverboat passengers and relieving them of their money. Cheating was rife.

Poker spread to the west with the settlers who travelled on wagon trains. When gold was discovered in California in 1848, gambling flourished in the prospecting camps. San Francisco, which became a huge tented city, had over 1000 gambling houses where gold was the currency. Initially, games like roulette were most popular but gradually card games like poker caught on.

The game spread rapidly during the Civil War (1861–65). Soldiers would play poker to pass the time. Lack of money resulted in their fashioning gaming chips out of flattened bullets and pieces of bone. The soldiers would usually discard their playing cards before battle as playing cards were considered to be 'instruments of the devil' and the soldiers did not want to die carrying them. It was during the Civil War that stud poker first emerged.

Many variations of the game started to appear that could be broadly divided into two types: draw poker and stud poker. In draw poker, all the cards are dealt face down and are seen only by the player of the hand. Players are then allowed to exchange cards to improve their hand. In stud poker, some of the cards are dealt face up on the table and players make a hand by combining their cards and those on the table. New rankings of hands and betting methods were also incorporated. In the 1867 edition of *Hoyles' Games*, a straight and a straight flush and an ante had been incorporated into the game. By 1875 jackpot poker and the use of a joker as a wildcard had been mentioned.

Poker players made a living travelling from town to town. Virtually every saloon of the Old West had a poker table where a buckhorn knife would be passed around the table to denote the dealer. This led to the phrase 'passing the buck'. Later, a silver dollar was used, which gave rise to the slang term of a buck for a dollar. Disputes over the game were often settled by gun. One famous poker player from this time was Doc Holliday (1851–87) who, on several occasions, got into a gunfight over poker.

Poker arrived in England in 1872. It was introduced by Robert C. Schenk, the American ambassador to England. He had been invited to a party at a country house in Somerset where he had taught his fellow guests how to play poker. The hostess persuaded him to write down the rules, which were then published. The game was popular among the aristocracy and became know as Schenk poker. Queen Victoria is known to have played the game as a diversion after the death of her husband, Prince Albert.

In 1911 legislation was passed in the United States that prohibited stud poker as it was concluded that it was a game of luck. However, a ruling was passed at the same time that draw poker was a game of skill and therefore not illegal. This led to the decline of stud poker and in new draw games being invented.

Prohibition in the 1920s was responsible for poker becoming a home-based game. With the closure of drinking and gaming establishments, private games were organized that became part of American culture. The traditional venue became the kitchen table where family and friends would gather to play. The playing of private games resulted in many variations appearing, with each household inventing its own rules. New rankings of hands, incorporation of one or more wildcards and different ways of organizing the betting appeared.

When gambling was legalized in Nevada in the 1930s, draw poker was introduced to Las Vegas casinos. In 1970 Benny Binion, owner of the Horseshoe Casino in Las Vegas, decided to hold a poker tournament so that the best players in the world could compete against one another. The tournament, called the World Series of Poker, has become an annual event with players from around the globe competing. The game chose for the championship was Texas hold 'em. This resulted in Texas hold 'em becoming one of the most widely played games.

In the mid-1980s Caribbean stud poker was invented on the Caribbean island of Aruba. It began to be played on cruise ships and gradually spread to casinos around the world. It differs from other poker games as it is played against the casino, which acts as banker. Instead of playing for a pot the winning hands are paid out at fixed odds. There is also no bluffing involved.

Poker has been played on gaming machines since the 1800s. In 1891 Sittman and Pitt of Brooklyn began manufacturing poker card machines. They proved extremely popular and were installed in virtually all Brooklyn's licensed liquor establishments, which at that time numbered over 3000. By 1901 the machines had been redesigned so that draw poker could be played.

In the mid-1970s video poker was invented. By 1976 the first black and white video poker machines appeared. They were superseded eight months later with a colour version. Nowadays video poker is one of the most popular casino games around.

With the innovation of the internet, online poker was invented. Computer technology allows players from all over the world to compete against one another from the comfort of their own homes. Gaming sites offer traditional poker, video poker and Caribbean stud poker.

Poker today

Poker is played around the world in private homes, casinos, card clubs and on the internet. It is estimated that poker is more popular than golf, fishing, football or basketball. The World Series of Poker attracts over 4000 players from around the world. A television audience of over 40 million watches the tournament. In Great Britain and Europe, there has been a rise in the popularity of poker, mostly due to tournaments being televised.

Casinos around the world offer a wide choice of poker games including five-card stud, seven-card stud, Texas hold 'em and Omaha. In addition, many more casinos have Caribbean stud poker, which is played as a banker game against the casino. Poker is also widely played on video poker machines. Around 10 per cent of visitors to Las Vegas casinos bet on video poker machines. This is more than play roulette, craps or keno. Poker is also played with dice as a pub game, which is particularly popular on continental Europe.

Famous poker players

In 1979 a hall of fame was founded to honour top poker players. Each year one player is added. Those winning the World Series gain entry. Other members have been given honorary membership. Players in the Poker Hall of Fame include:

Benny Binion (1904–89) – a former cowboy, gambler and owner of the Horseshoe Casino, the venue for the World Series. He was an all-round player, skilled at many forms of poker.

Doyle 'Texas Dolly' Brunson (1933–) – he gave up a career as a salesman to become a professional poker player in the 1950s when he realized that he could earn ten times his salary in a fraction of the time at the tables. He practised the game for up to 20 hours a day and started out playing in backroom card games. He won $600,000 as winner of the World Series in two consecutive years in 1976 and 1977.

'Nick 'the Greek' Dandolos (1893–1966) – became famous for his huge bets. His gambling career started after he won $500,000 in six months betting on horse racing. He then took up card and dice games where he lost his fortune.

Undaunted, he decided to study card games and reportedly won over $6 million at stud poker throughout his career.

'Wild Bill' Hickok (1837–1876) – a poker player with a short but eventful life. He was a scout during the Civil War, a marshal in Kansas and toured in Buffalo Bill's Wild West Show as a sharpshooter. He was shot in the back during a poker game by Crooked Nose McCall on 2 August 1876. The hand that he was holding at the time, a pair of aces over eights, has gone down in poker legend as the dead man's hand.

Johnny Moss (1907–1997) – three times winner of the World Series in 1970, 1971 and 1974. He once played a five-month long game with Nick the Greek, only taking breaks for sleep. Moss won an estimated $2 million in this game.

02

playing tips

In this chapter you will learn:
- how to stay solvent
- about the costs of playing
- how to recognize gambling problems.

Taking a sensible approach

Before you begin gambling, you should work out a financial budget. Calculate all your household and living costs including savings. Work out how much money you can realistically, and comfortably, afford to lose – yes, lose. Gambling is risky, not everyone wins, and there are plenty of losers. You can easily lose all your capital. Be aware that there are much easier, more profitable and safer ways of making money.

Once you have decided on your budget, make sure you *never* go over this limit. If your personal circumstances change, be sure to recalculate. If you spend only disposable income on gambling, you won't encounter many problems. However, if you start betting with your rent money and lose it, you may be tempted to try to recoup your losses by betting more heavily. This is the route to financial ruin.

When you play, take only your stake money and enough for your expenses (fare home, drinks, meals etc.). Leave all cheque books and cash cards at home. If you can't get hold of more money, you can't spend it. Don't be tempted to borrow money from friends and be sure to decline all offers of credit. If you run out of money, either go home or just watch.

If you don't want to carry large amounts of cash, open a separate account for your gambling money and take with you only the cheque book and cards relating to that account when you gamble.

Exchanging money for chips

In most games, particularly in casinos, you exchange your money for chips. You don't play with 'real money', just a pile of plastic discs. Psychologically, the value of your money diminishes. When you see a banknote, you associate it with its true value – you appreciate how long it would take you to earn that amount of money and what you can buy with it. As soon as you exchange it for chips, those associations disappear. It is no accident that chips resemble coins – coins are considered almost worthless. It's easy to pick up a pile of chips and put them on a bet. If you had to count out banknotes, you would certainly be more cautious.

When you decide to play, don't immediately change all your money into chips. Instead, change it in small amounts. If you have to keep going to your wallet, you will have a better appreciation of how much you are losing as you will be watching real money diminish rather than chips.

If you win, it's all too easy to give your winnings back by continuing to play. If you are playing in a casino, as soon as is convenient, go to the cashpoint and change your cash chips back into money. Once you see the true value, you will be more reluctant to carry on betting.

People like to have piles of chips in front of them – it makes them look like a high roller. Walk around a casino and see the proud smiles when someone has a big pile of chips. However, you should only have in front of you the amount of chips that you need to play. Lots of high-denomination chips on the table are an incentive for thieves to steal them.

Games on the internet are played at a much faster pace than traditional games. It is therefore possible to lose your money at a much faster rate. Placing a bet does not even involve the handling of chips. You simply click on your computer mouse. Often there is a time limit placed on how long you have to make a decision. You will be making decisions to bet or raise in a few seconds, which does not allow you the opportunity to give much thought to your decision. As soon as one game is over, the next starts immediately.

What does it cost to play?

Once you have calculated your budget you need to find a game that is compatible with your level of stakes. If the stakes are too high, you will find yourself quickly running out of money.

The minimum amount of capital you need varies depending on the game and where you play. As a rough guide, the capital needed for a game of draw poker is around 40 times the minimum stake. With seven-card stud it is approximately 50 times the minimum stake, while games like Texas hold 'em and Omaha need around 100 times the minimum stake.

Private games tend to be played at a slow pace with around 10 to 15 rounds an hour. This is because the players tend to be less experienced at dealing and shuffling the cards than casino dealers. The games tend to be informal with a more relaxed atmosphere and more banter. Players may be given more time to make decisions. Playing a £1 game of Omaha for an hour in a private game would cost you approximately £1000.

In casinos, you can expect from 25 to 40 hands per hour. Casinos use professional dealers who will deal the cards in a fast and efficient manner. The players are strangers so conversation is kept to a minimum. Players are expected to make quick decisions. Playing a £1 game of Omaha for an hour in a casino would cost you from about £2500.

On the internet the games are even faster with over 60 hands per hour. This is because the cards are not physically dealt. The hands are dealt by computer software that takes less than a second to deal the cards. Playing a £1 game of Omaha for an hour on the internet could cost around £6000.

You can calculate your stake level by dividing the amount that you have budgeted for by the minimum capital required and the number of games you want to play.

The minimum stake on many poker games is low. You should be able to find somewhere to play to suit your budget. You don't have to be a high roller to go to a casino. Most casinos have plenty of low-stake tables. If you prefer to play in private games, you should be able to find one that suits your level of stakes, while on the internet stakes start as low as £0.01.

Do not aim too high when you are still learning. Even if your budget allows you to play in the more expensive games, stick initially to the cheaper games and gradually work your way up. Remember, the higher the stakes the better the players.

Additional costs

It's all too easy to go over your budget by forgetting to include all the costs. Casino gambling has additional costs, including:

• house advantage
• commission
• admission charges
• memberships fees
• travelling costs
• refreshments
• your time.

House advantage

In games where the casino acts as a banker, a hidden charge is made for the privilege of betting. Many people don't even realize that there is a charge for gambling. On many games like Caribbean stud poker and pai gow poker you are not paid the true odds. The casinos reduces the odds paid to allow it to make a profit. This profit is called the house advantage. On Caribbean stud poker the casino makes on average a 5.26 per cent profit by correspondingly reducing the odds it pays.

Commission

Casinos charge the gambler for the use of their facilities. They have to maintain premises, employ staff and buy gaming equipment. With poker, a percentage of the pot is taken by the house. This is a small price to pay when you consider that you are guaranteed a fairly, professionally run games. Around 10 per cent is the usual deduction. For bigger games, players are often charged an hourly rate for their seat.

Finding your game

It is a good idea to try playing a variety of games at home. Decide which game you like the most and, once you have selected your favourite, concentrate solely on that game. Try to watch as many games as possible – you can learn a great deal by watching experienced players. If someone is winning, try to determine why. Are they just lucky or are they using a particular strategy? Are their stakes varied or constant? What do they do when they lose – do they increase or reduce their stakes or stop playing?

Check the rules before you start playing

Learn how to play a game before you bet on it. This may seem common sense, but a lot of people start playing poker with no understanding of the rules. Often they are introduced to poker by friends or relations and they simply bet in the same manner as their friends. They end up learning by their mistakes, which can be costly.

Remember, the rules of poker vary enormously. Ensure you fully understand all the rules before you play. Casinos will have written copies of their rules available. Take them home and study them at your leisure. If you don't understand them, ask for an explanation. Whatever game you select, find out as much information about it as possible.

You need to be particularly careful with private games, as rules may differ enormously. Just knowing the name of a game is not sufficient, as players often introduce variations.

Have a full discussion about the rules before you start playing. It is often a good idea to write down the rules that you have been told to avoid disputes later about what was actually said before play commences.

Pay particular attention to the ranking of hands as you may find that hands other than the standard rankings are permitted. Ensure that you fully understand the method of betting and whether or not checking is allowed (see page 20). Agree both minimum and maximum bets. If wildcards are used, check if additional hands like five of a kind count in the ranking.

The lollapalooza

John Lillard's *Poker Stories* (1896) recounts the tale of a cheat playing a game of poker in a Montana saloon. He deals himself a hand of four aces and ends up betting against an old prospector. The prospector bets all his money against the cheat. When the hands are revealed the prospector has only an assortment of clubs and diamonds, which is not a ranking poker hand. The cheat starts counting his winnings, only to be stopped by the old man. He explains that a lollapalooza beats any other poker hand and that three clubs and two diamonds is, in fact, a lollapalooza. The other players agree with him so the cheat concedes the win. Later in the game, the cheat deals himself a lollapalooza. He bets heavily on his hand. At the showdown he reveals his hand expecting to take the pot. He is then informed that he should ask the rules before playing as a lollapalooza can only be played once a night.

Get plenty of practice

You need to be able to correctly identify a poker hand and recognize immediately the value of your hand and where it comes in the ranking. When you first look at your cards they may appear to show nothing, they will be in a random order and it may at first not be obvious that you have, for example, a straight or a possibility of a straight. At the showdown, you will need to know, for example, that your full house beats a flush.

To get better at recognizing the hands you can practise assessing the hands by dealing out dummy hands. Deal out hands of five cards, identify the poker hands and put them in the correct ranking order. You will soon appreciate how infrequently a good hand is dealt. Once you have mastered the ranking, you can then start to judge whether or not a hand is worth playing.

Get plenty of practice. As a beginner, first learn how to play five-card stud. Start out with playing dummy five-card stud hands. Take a pack of cards and deal out dummy hands as if you're playing the game with several players. Look at your own hand. Decide whether or not it is worth playing. Then assess your hand against the others. Did you make a good decision? Would any of the other hands have beaten yours? Are you throwing away hands that could easily win? By continuing to do this, you will learn the sort of hands that are worthwhile playing and those that are not.

When you have mastered five-card stud, graduate to five-card draw. This is a simple game that will help you to appreciate the chances of improving on a hand with further cards. Play dummy five-card draw hands. Assess your hand and decide if it is worth playing. Exchange cards as if in a real game. Do the same with the other players' hands then compare the results. This will help you to determine which hands are good for improving and which are not.

With a greater understanding of how extra cards can improve a hand, you can then try out seven-card stud, Texas hold 'em and omaha. These games are more complex, with greater possibilities for higher ranking hands and more betting rounds.

Play alone or with friends until you are familiar with all situations. Practise placing bets as you play. Some games are played so quickly that it can be difficult for a novice to follow them. With practice you will become faster.

As mentioned earlier, it is important to play at the right level. Don't aim too high when you are still learning. Stick to the simpler, cheaper games and gradually work your way up. Remember the higher the stakes the better the players.

Other considerations

Poker relies on the other players not knowing your hand. Although the other players cannot see your hand, the way that you react to its contents can give them a lot of information.

Body language

Suppose you have a really good hand. It is quite likely that, as you look at the cards, you will smile, raise your eyebrows or constantly look at your cards. You know that this time you are certain of a winning hand. When you're anxious or excited your voice also changes. The other players will notice and probably fold, meaning that your good hand will win you very little money.

If, alternatively, you have a poor hand, you are more likely to frown. You may decide to try bluffing, but if you appear nervous and fidgety, the other players are less likely to believe you. You may even give one of the classic signs of lying, such as touching your nose. When you are nervous, you are also more likely to stutter.

People who have complete control over their mannerisms make better poker players. If you can look at your cards and show no facial expression whatsoever you make it impossible for other players to glean any information about your hand. When you look at your hand, memorize its contents. Pay attention to your mannerisms – don't fiddle with your chips or your jewellery. Stay calm, even if you have a royal flush. If you play and bet confidently you are more likely to intimidate the other player. See Chapter 7 for a more detailed look at body language.

Keep records

Keep records of your gambling. A small notebook is sufficient to keep records of how much you win and lose. Most people tend to remember the big wins and forget the losses. After each game, write down the reasons why you won or lost. Analyse the results and learn from your mistakes.

If you lost, try to determine why. Were you staying in when you should have folded? Were you folding with hands that could have won? Were you failing to force other players into folding? Was your body language giving away information?

When you win also try to determine the reasons why. Was it because your strategy was good? Were you just dealt lots of good hands? Did other players make stupid mistakes? Were you picking up on any signs given by the other players?

Periodically analyse your records. They will tell you if you're sticking to your budget and if your betting strategy is effective. Proper records will make you aware of any weaknesses. You can then alter your strategy to compensate.

Player profiles

If you play regularly with the same people, try to build up a profile of each one.

- What sort of hands do they bet heavily on?
- What forces them to fold?
- How often do they bluff?
- Does their body language give any clues?
- How do they bet with a good hand?

Players use different styles of play. Some play aggressively, continually raising in an attempt to force everyone to fold. Other players are very cautious, throwing away anything that is not a good hand. You will know when they suddenly make a huge bet they have a good hand. Try to work out each player's strategy.

Appreciate your chances of winning

Many people expect to win but don't realistically assess their chances of winning. With all bets there is the chance that you will lose and it is important to understand how to calculate your chances of winning. You may decide that a bet is simply not worthwhile.

Learn how to calculate the odds for the game that you are playing. Learn how to calculate the chances of getting your desired hand and compare this with the stakes you bet, the potential pot and the chances of other hands beating yours. Fully appreciate your chances of improving hands. Before you place a bet, make sure you understand your chances of winning. If you are playing in a casino, do not forget to take into account the rake.

With banking games find both the true odds (your chances of winning) and the odds paid by the casino. Is there a huge difference? You may decide that it is not worth your while having a bet.

Vary your play

Try not to stick to one style of playing. The most successful poker players are those who are totally unpredictable. If in some hands you play cautiously and in others aggressively, you will confuse the opposition. You should aim to vary your betting, the number of cards you take (if playing a draw game), how often you bluff and the signals that you give off.

Know when to stop gambling

It can take an enormous amount of discipline to stop betting, particularly if you are on a winning streak. It is possible to get carried away by the excitement of the game. You may have intended to spend only an hour gambling but you're on a winning streak, so you continue. Because you are betting with your winnings rather than the initial stake money, you decide to place larger bets. Your next best loses, what do you do? For some people, the tendency is to bet more heavily to recoup that loss. This will usually continue until you run out of funds.

If you have lost your stake money, decline all offers of credit. Private poker games are particularly susceptible to players losing more money than they intended. You may play with friends who will be happy to lend you money or extend you credit. Even if the other players agree to accept an IOU, you should withdraw from the game. Stories abound of people who have run out of money and who have ended up throwing their jewellery, car keys or the promise of some other asset into the pot.

If the stakes are getting too high or you are losing too much, stop playing. By having a sensible approach to gambling you can ensure that you do not lose more than you can afford.

Try to decide in advance at what stage you are going to stop betting. Set yourself an amount to win or lose or impose a time limit. Stop playing when you have reached your limit. As soon as a winning streak stops, either bet small stakes or go home.

This approach will minimize your losses. Other players may complain if you suddenly stop playing, but remember you are not betting for their benefit. Do not feel obliged to give them the opportunity to win their money back.

You should always stop playing if you are tired. You need to ensure that you are concentrating on the game. When you are tired, you take longer to make decisions and are more likely to make mistakes.

It is also wise to avoid alcohol. It tends to slow down your reactions and your ability to think. It also lowers your inhibitions and makes you less likely to care about losses. You should certainly never play if you are drunk.

Staying in control

The majority of gamblers are able to keep to their budgets and bet without its becoming a problem. However, for some people it can become addictive, leading to financial ruin and family breakdown. If you start losing more than you can afford, seek help.

You can recognize that you have a problem if you:

- view betting as a way of earning money
- continually exceed your budget
- bet money that was intended for living costs
- borrow money for betting
- take days off work to bet
- spend all your free time betting
- find your betting interferes with family life.

There are organizations that can offer solutions. Many have a telephone helpline where you speak to a councillor. They also hold meetings where gamblers can discuss their problems and find solutions. There are also organizations that support gamblers' families. Your general practitioner will also be able to offer advice on counselling. Details of organizations that can help are given at the end of the book.

Some casinos also offer self-exclusion schemes. During the period of self-exclusion they will not take bets from you.

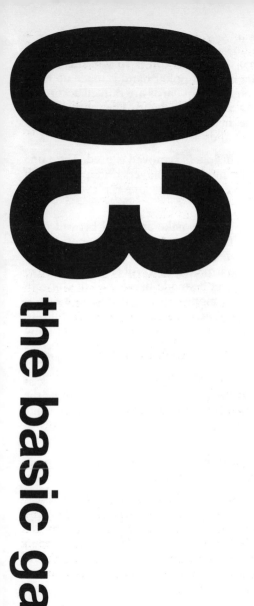

03

the basic game

In this chapter you will learn:
- about the basics of poker
- about ranking of the hands
- about additional rankings.

Basics

Poker is a gambling game where the aim is to win the pot by having the highest ranking hand. A poker hand is made up from five cards. Different combinations of cards are ranked according to the chances of acquiring a particular hand. The more difficult a hand is to achieve, the higher its position in the ranking. Figure 3.2 shows how the hands are ranked.

One deck of 52 cards with the jokers removed is used. The game can be played with a minimum of two players and a maximum of 10, depending on which version of the game is played. Players take turns to be the dealer.

Before any cards are dealt, players make an initial bet called an ante-bet, or ante for short. This helps to increase the pot. It also makes the game more competitive as players are more likely to try to win the pot if they have contributed to it. All bets are placed in the centre of the table. Bets can be made using cash or chips. In casinos, players exchange their money for chips. In private games, bets are often made with cash but some schools may use chips to facilitate betting. Instead of making an ante-bet, a round of blind betting may take place. One or more players makes a bet before looking at their cards. This is also a means of increasing the pot.

Each player receives five cards dealt face down. Players look at their cards. A round of betting commences starting with the player to the left of the dealer (in forms of poker where some cards are placed face up, the player with the highest or lowest card may bet first).

Each player has the option of betting or folding (withdrawing from the game). A player holding a poor hand may decide to fold. If you fold, your cards are returned to the dealer without being revealed to the other players. You lose any bets made. The cards no longer in play are put in a separate pile from the other cards. This pile of folded cards is called the muck pile.

Some games allow players to 'check'. This usually happens on the first round of betting after the cards have been dealt. Instead of betting, players announce 'check'. They do not contribute any money to the pot. If they wish to continue in the game they must bet on their next turn. If all the players decide to check, new hands are dealt to everyone.

The first bet determines how much each player has to bet in order to stay in the game. Betting continues clockwise around the table. Each subsequent player must bet at least as much as the previous player to stay in the game. Players may also raise the bet up to the agreed maximum. When a bet is raised, players must decide whether or not to match the raise to stay in the game or to fold. As betting progresses more players may fold. If all the other players fold and only one player is left in the game, the remaining player wins the pot. He does not reveal his cards to the other players.

If all players have matched the last bet and there are no further raises a showdown occurs. All the remaining players turn their cards face up. Players' hands are then compared. The player with the highest ranking poker hand wins the pot. In the event of a tie, the pot is shared. Figure 3.1 shows various poker hands. In a showdown, player D would win as he has the highest ranking hand.

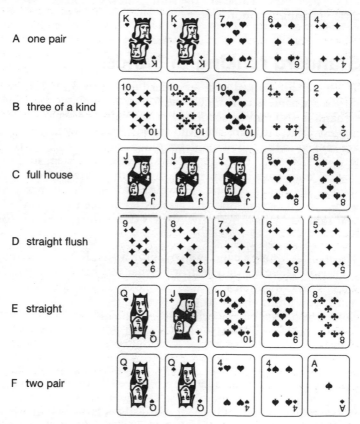

A	one pair
B	three of a kind
C	full house
D	straight flush
E	straight
F	two pair

figure 3.1 example hands

The basic game of poker is easy to learn. This is poker in its simplest form, but it is hardly ever played in this manner. Many variations have been introduced to make the games more exciting and challenging. There is a huge number of different games where both the rules and the method of betting vary. Games of the same name may be played in a huge variety of ways in different locations. Gamblers who play regularly together may also add their own rules to create more excitement. The number of cards dealt to each player varies with different games. Some games allow players to improve their hands by taking extra cards, these are the draw games. Other forms exist where some cards are placed face up on the table. Either some of the player's cards are revealed or players use community cards combined with their own cards to make up the best hand. These are the stud games. Chapter 9 describes different games in more detail.

Standard ranking of hands

The hands are ranked in a set order (see Figure 3.2). The more difficult a hand is to achieve, the higher its ranking. Each type of hand is also ranked according to the values of the cards. The highest value cards are aces and the lowest are twos. The cards are ranked in the following descending order: A, K, Q, J, 10, 9, 8, 7, 6, 5, 4, 3, 2. The suits do not affect the ranking, so if two players both have a royal flush, one with hearts and one with spades, the hands will tie. However, if you play in a private game, you may find that the players introduce their own rules that rank the suits differently. Always check the rankings before you play.

The highest ranking hand is a royal flush – A, K, Q, J, 10 in the same suit. There are only four ways that this hand can be made, with hearts, diamonds, spades or clubs. If you are dealt this hand, you know that you have the highest ranking hand and cannot be beaten by any other player. The only other possibility is that another player may have a royal flush and therefore tie with you.

A straight flush is a run of five cards of the same suit in consecutive numerical order. It two players both have a straight flush, the player with the highest card wins so Kc, Qc, Jc, 10c, 9c beats Qh, Jh, 10h, 9h, 8h. If two players both have the same straight flush with different suits, the hand is a tie and the pot is shared.

royal flush

straight flush

four of a kind

full house

flush

straight

three of a kind

two pair

one pair

no pair, highest card

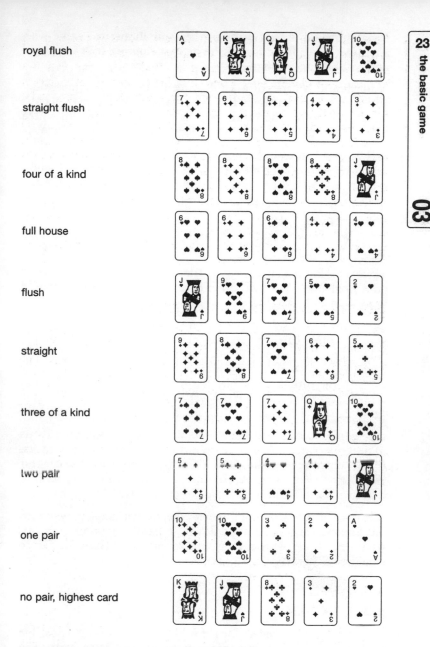

figure 3.2 poker hands ranked from highest to lowest

Four of a kind is four cards of the same numerical value with any other card. Four aces is the highest ranking four of a kind and will beat four kings.

A full house is three of a kind (three cards of the same value) and a pair (two cards of the same value). Where two players have a full house, the hand with the highest value for the three of a kind wins. So 10, 10, 10, 2, 2, would beat 8, 8, 8, A, A.

A flush is a run of five cards of the same suit in any numerical order. Where two players have a flush, the one with the highest card wins. So Js, 8s, 6s, 5s, 3s would beat 9d, 8d, 6d, 5d, 4d.

A straight is five cards of any suit in consecutive numerical order. A, K, Q, J, 10 is the highest straight followed by K, Q, J, 10, 9. Where two players both have a straight, the hand with the highest card wins.

Three of a kind, also known as trips, is three cards of the same numerical value with two other cards. 6h, 6d, 6c, 8h, 5d would beat 4d, 4s, 4c, Ad, Kh.

Two pair is two sets of pairs (two cards with the same value) with any other card. Where two players both have two pair, the value of the highest pair decides the winner. A, A, 3, 3, 2 would beat 10, 10, 8, 8, A. If both players have the same two pair, the value of the fifth card decides the winner. K, K, Q, Q, 8 would beat K, K, Q, Q, 4. If two players both have cards of the same value there is a tie and the pot is shared.

One pair is two cards of the same value with three other cards of different values. A pair of queens would beat a pair of jacks. If two players have the same pair, the hand with the highest value other cards wins. A, A, 10, 7, 5 would beat A, A, 9, 7, 5. If all cards are of the same value, there is a tie.

Where none of these hands is held, the winner is the player with the highest card. In a showdown, a hand containing an ace would beat one with a king and so on. Qh, 10h, 7d, 3s, 2c would beat Jd, 10s, 4c, 3h, 2s.

Low poker

The ranking described so far is for high poker. It is also possible to play low poker, where the lowest ranking hand wins. The lowest hand is 5, 4, 3, 2, A and is known as the 'wheel' or the 'bicycle'.

the 'wheel'
or 'bicycle'

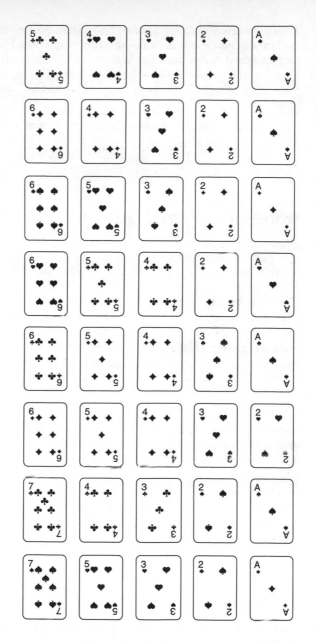

figure 3.3 ranking of hands in low poker

Although this would be a straight in high poker, straights and flushes do not exist in low poker. Other games exist where players compete for both the highest hand and the lowest hand. They usually nominate what hand they are playing for. Here the pot will be split, half for the highest hand and half for the lowest hand.

Figure 3.3 shows how the low hands are ranked. Before playing these games, you should check what the lowest rankings are, as they may vary. Aces are the lowest cards followed by twos, threes, fours etc. with kings as the highest.

Additional rankings

It is always important to check the ranking of the hands before you play as some private games include additional hands. Some of the more commonly found hands are now described. However, this list is not comprehensive and a private game could conceivably contain virtually any other hand. You should always therefore check exactly what is and is not permitted.

Skeet/pelter/bracket

These hands come between a flush and a straight in the ranking. It is commonly 9, 5, 2 and two other cards below 9 of any combination of suits. However, some games specify that the two other cards must include one card between 9 and 5 and the other card between 5 and 2. If the cards are all the same suit, you have a skeet flush which ranks higher than a straight flush.

Dutch/skip straight or kilter

This is an alternately numbered straight. For example, 10, 8, 6, 4, 2 or K, J, 9, 7, 5. It ranks lower than a straight but higher than three of a kind.

Blaze

This is a combination of any five court cards that do not contain three of a kind. For example, K, K, Q, Q, J or Q, Q, J, J, K. It ranks higher than two pair but lower than three of a kind. Where this hand is allowed it would, for example, beat A, A, 9, 9, 7.

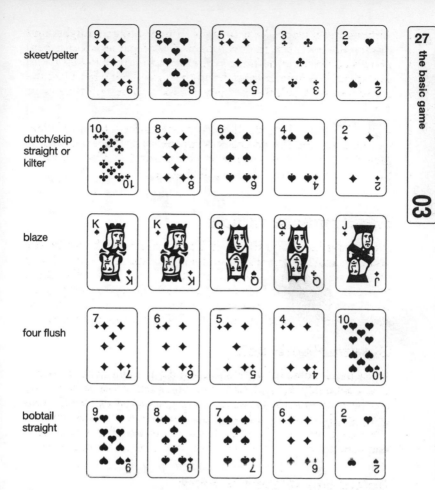

figure 3.4 additional rankings

Four flush

This hand consists of four cards of the same suit, for example, 7d, 6d, 5d, 4d, 10c. It ranks higher than a pair and lower than two pair.

Bobtail straight

This hand consists of four consecutive cards of any suit and ranks below a four flush. For example 9h, 8s, 7s, 6d, 2h.

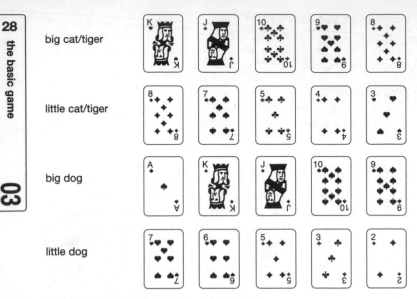

big cat/tiger

little cat/tiger

big dog

little dog

figure 3.5 additional rankings – cats and dogs

Cats and dogs

The following hands rank between a flush and a straight. If they are permitted, always check exactly where they come in the ranking as their position may vary. None of the hands may contain a pair. (See Figure 3.5 for examples.)

Big cat/tiger

This hand consists of a king and an 8 with three other cards with a value between a king and an 8.

Little cat/tiger

This hand should have an 8 and a 3 with the three other cards having a value between 8 and a 3.

Big dog

This hand needs an ace and a 9 with three other cards having a value between an ace and a 9.

Little dog

This hand consists of a 7 and a 2 with the three other cards having a value between 7 and 2.

Round the corner straight

This is a straight that has cards on both sides of the ace for example 4, 3, 2, A, K or 3, 2, A, K, Q. It ranks lower than a straight but higher than three of a kind.

Five and dime

This is a 5 and a 10 with three other cards having a value between 5 and 10.

Ranking hands with wildcards

In private games, it is common to allow the use of wildcards. A wildcard is a nominated card that may be used in the place of any other card. For example, the twos may be declared 'wild'. If you needed an ace to make up a hand, you could use a 2 instead of an ace. Alternatively, one or more jokers may be added to the pack and declared wild. If, for example, you needed a queen to make up a hand, you could use the joker in its place. By allowing cards to be wild, higher ranking hands are easier to achieve. If the twos are wild, then Jh, Jd, 2h, 7c, 3s would be a hand of three of a kind with jacks, where the two becomes a jack. If the joker is wild, then a hand of 10h, 10d, 10c, Ah, joker would be four of a kind with tens. The joker becomes a 10.

Playing with wildcards can lead to a number of disputes over the ranking of the hands. This is because it is possible to make hands that do not appear in the standard ranking, such as five of a kind. It is also possible for players to have identical hands – the same three of a kind or the same full house.

Five of a kind

When wildcards are allowed, an additional hand of five of a kind is also possible (see Figure 3.6). Five of a kind ranks higher than a royal flush. If you are playing with wildcards always check that five of a kind is permitted as some games may specify that the wildcard may only be used in place of another card that excludes this possibility. For example, if, you have four of a kind with aces and your fifth card is an ace, the hand will be four aces and not five of a kind.

five of a kind with jokers wild

five of a kind with twos wild

figure 3.6 five of a kind

Three of a kind

With wildcards it is possible for two players to both have three of a kind. For example, in a game where twos are wild, you may have the following hands in a showdown:

Player A – K, K, K, Q, 5
Player B – K, 2, 2, 10, 6

Both players have three of a kind with kings. In this situation, you would take the other cards into consideration. Player A's next highest card is a queen. Player B's next highest card is a 10. Since a queen is higher than a 10, player A has the higher hand.

Ranking of suits

The suits are not normally ranked in poker. However, a private game may do so. Where the ranking of the suits is taken into account the order of is usually spades, hearts, diamond, clubs where spades are the highest and clubs the lowest. Other rankings may also be used, so always check the rules before playing.

Cards speak

Is it common practice in a poker game to include a rule that cards speak. This means that the player will have whatever hand the cards show and not the hand that the player declares.

A player may make a mistake about the hand held. For example, he may announce that he has a straight when, in fact, a straight flush is held. In this case, the hand of a straight flush is what counts in a showdown.

Example

Player A: Jh, 10h, 9h, 8h, 7h
Player B: Q, Q, Q, 10, 10

Player A announces that he has a straight and player B that he has a full house. Player A will still win as he actually has a straight flush. It is up to the other players to point out his fault. He may also correct himself.

04

understanding the odds

In this chapter you will learn:
- the odds of poker
- how the odds change with different games
- the effect of using wildcards.

In order to play poker well, a sound understanding of the odds of being dealt particular hands is essential. With this knowledge, you can then decide if your hand is worthwhile playing or should be folded. Different games have different odds of achieving ranking hands. With games like draw poker, you need to know the chances of improving your hand. You also need to understand the chances of the other players having hands that could beat yours. As private games incorporate so many variations, it is important to understand how changes in the rules affect the odds. The inclusion of wildcards has a big effect on the odds of getting particular hands.

In standard games of poker, 52 cards are used to make five card hands. There are 2,598,960 different possible hands that can be dealt.

$$\frac{52 \times 51 \times 50 \times 49 \times 48}{1 \times 2 \times 3 \times 4 \times 5} = 2,598,960$$

Hand	Number of ways hand can be made	Odds against being dealt cards in your first hand
Royal flush	4	649,739/1
Straight flush	36	72,192/1
Four of a kind	624	4,164/1
Full house	3,744	693/1
Flush	5,108	508/1
Straight	10,200	254/1
Three of a kind	54,912	46/1
Two pair	123,552	20/1
One pair	1,098,240	15/1
Highest card	1,302,540	1/1

table 4.1 the likelihood of being dealt a particular hand in poker

To appreciate just how rare the higher ranking hands are, when only five cards are dealt consider how long it takes to play 649,740 hands (the chances of being dealt a royal flush). If you play, for example, an average of one hand every five minutes, you would need to continue playing constantly for approximately six years and two months. By playing for a few hours each week, the chances of being dealt a royal flush in your first hand are nothing short of a miracle.

Take a pack of cards and deal them out into five-card poker hands. By continually repeating this, you will begin to appreciate just how rare it is to be dealt one of the higher ranking hands. You will start to get some idea about which hands are worth playing. Pairs are very common. Pairs appear very low down in the ranking but a high pair can often be sufficient to win a game like five-card stud.

If poker is played with only five cards and no further cards exchanged for others from the pack, players are mostly competing with low-ranking hands. This is one of the main reasons why so many variations of poker exist. By increasing the number of cards dealt to each player or allowing players to exchange some of the cards for new ones from the pack, the chances of having a higher ranking hand are increased. The varied games add more interest and excitement.

How the odds change with different games

Poker can be played in a wide variety of ways. A different number of cards may be dealt and the number of cards players can exchange may vary. To have a good knowledge of the odds for your particular game you need to take these factors into consideration in your calculations. Before agreeing to any changes in the rules, ensure that you fully appreciate how the change will affect the odds.

Draw games

When you are playing draw poker, you have the opportunity to improve your hand by exchanging your cards for others from the deck. Before betting and exchanging cards, you will want to know your chances of improving your hand so that you can decide if it is worthwhile staying in the game.

You can calculate your chances of improving your hand by comparing the number of ways in which your desired cards can be dealt to the number of possible ways in which the remaining cards can be dealt.

Chances of improving a hand when three of a kind is held

Suppose your hand is K, K, K, 6, 3. By exchanging your last two cards, you have the opportunity to make either a full house or four of a kind. For the full house, you need a pair and for four of a kind another king is required.

There are four cards of the same value in each suit. To achieve a pair, each value can be arranged in six different ways (see Figure 4.1).

figure 4.1 ways in which a pair of fours can be made

There are 13 different values in total, from ace to 2. As you already hold the kings, you are left with a possible 12 other values from which to make a pair. A pair can be made in 72 ways (6 × 12 = 72). You are discarding two cards, which reduces the number of ways a pair can be made by five. You therefore have 72 − 5 = 67 ways in which you can make a full house.

You currently hold five cards, leaving 47 other possible cards (52 − 5 = 47). Even though some of the other cards have been dealt to other players, you do not know what cards they hold, so you need to take all possibilities into account when making your calculations. With 47 cards there are 1081 ways in which two cards can be dealt:

$$\frac{47 \times 46}{1 \times 2} = 1081$$

Your chances of improving your hand to make a full house are (1081 − 67)/67 or 1009/67 or odds of approximately 15/1.

To improve the hand to four of a kind you need the last king. By exchanging one card, you are giving yourself odds of 46/1. By exchanging two cards, your odds of having the king are 46/2 or 23/1.

Chances of making four of a kind by drawing three cards to a pair

Suppose your hand is A, A, 7, 9, 4. With three cards there are a possible 16,215 hands:

$$\frac{47 \times 46 \times 45}{1 \times 2 \times 3} = 16{,}215$$

The hand you want to be dealt is A, A, X where 'X' is any other card. A, A, X can be made in 45 ways, where 'X' is any of the other 45 cards.

Your chances of being dealt this hand are (16215 − 45)/45 or 359/1. You can see that the chances of making this hand are remote.

Chances of making a full house by drawing one card to two pair

If Q, Q, J, J, 10 is held, you need either a queen or a jack for a full house. You exchange one card. There are 47 possible cards that could be dealt to you. Four of them would give you the desired hand (the other two jacks or the other two queens) − 43 of them would not. The odds are 43/4 = 10.75/1.

Chances of making a flush when one card is needed

Suppose your hand is K, 9, 4, 2 of hearts and 10 of diamonds. Your chances of getting another heart to make the flush are as follows: there are nine hearts left that would give you the desired hand and 38 other cards. Your chances of having a heart are 38/9 = 4.33/1.

There is a general rule about draw poker that says if you get nothing in your first deal you should fold. If you study the table odds for improving hands you can see the reasoning behind this rule. You may dream of turning a pair into four of a kind but in reality, it is very difficult to achieve.

Stud games

In games like seven-card stud and Texas hold 'em, a five-card poker hand is made from seven cards. With seven cards you are able to make up 21 different five card poker hands:

$$\frac{7 \times 6 \times 5 \times 4 \times 3}{1 \times 2 \times 3 \times 4 \times 5} = 21$$

This hugely improves each player's chances of achieving a higher ranking hand. By looking at the cards that each player is showing or the community cards, you can deduce the possible hand that they may hold and calculate the chances of their having that particular hand.

With Omaha, nine cards are used to make a five-card poker hand. Therefore, 60 different five-card poker hands can be made by each player, which makes it even easier to achieve a high-ranking poker hand.

Therefore, note that a pair of aces may have been enough to win a game of five card stud, but in Omaha, a pair of aces is highly likely to be beaten.

You are also able to adjust any calculations about players' hands by taking into account the cards that you hold and those the other players have on display. Consider a game of seven card stud, where four cards of each player's hand are displayed.

A player may have two queens and two jacks displayed. In order to make a full house, he needs either another jack or another queen in his hand. If you have a queen in your hand and another player has a jack displayed, then a full house with queens and jacks can only be made from two other cards, the remaining jack or queen.

If there are five players, 20 cards are displayed and you also have three cards in your hand. That leaves 29 other cards. Two cards would give a full house. This means that the player has odds of 13.5/1 against having a full house (29 −2)/2 = 13.5/1.

If no jacks or queens were displayed by other players or in your hand, the odds against his having a full house with jacks and queens would be (29 − 4)/4 = 6.25/1. You can see that taking into account the cards you hold or those displayed by other players can make a big difference to the odds.

Texas hold 'em odds

AA	220/1
AK suited	331/1
AK	110/1
Any pair	16/1
Two cards J or higher	10/1
Ace	5.25/1
Two cards suited	3.25/1
Any pair of ace's	3.9/1

table 4.2 odds of getting particular pocket cards

Pocket pair to three of a kind on the flop	7/1
Pocket no pair to a pair on the flop	2/1
Pocket A, K, A or K by the river	Evens
Two pair on flop to a full house	5/1
Three of a kind on flop to a full house or four of a kind	3/2
Completing a four flush	3/2
Completing open-ended straight flush to flush or straight by river	0.85/1
Completing open-ended straight	2/1
One pair on flop to two pair or three of a kind by river	4/1

table 4.3 odds of improving hands

How the odds are calculated

Odds of getting pocket aces

There are four aces in a deck, which can be dealt in six different ways to make a pair of aces. Figure 4.1 shows the ways that a pair can be dealt.

The four aces can be dealt six ways:

$$\frac{4 \times 3}{1 \times 2} = 6$$

From 52 cards, 1326 two card hands can be dealt.

$$\frac{52 \times 51}{1 \times 2} = 1326$$

$$1326/6 = 221.$$

The odds of getting pocket aces are therefore 220/1.

Odds of getting any pair

There are 13 possible pairs and each pair can be dealt six ways:

1326/(13 × 6) = 17

The odds of getting any pair are 16/1.

Calculating the odds of improving on your hand

Suppose you have a pair of queens and you want to calculate the odds of getting a third queen on the flop; there are two queens and 48 other cards in the deck. There are three cards dealt in the flop, giving you three chances to get a queen. Your odds of getting a queen are 7/1: (52 − 2 − 2)/48 × 3 = 8 which is odds of 7/1.

Pot odds

The pot odds is the odds that you are getting for making a bet. For example, if there is £50 in the pot and you need to make a bet of £5 to stay in the game, you are getting odds of 10/1.

By comparing the odds to achieve a particular hand with the pot odds, you can decide whether or not it is worthwhile making a bet.

To make a bet worthwhile, the pot odds would need to be higher than the odds of achieving a winning hand. Suppose the pot odds are 10/1 and the odds of your making a hand that you assess is sufficient to win are 4/1, it is worthwhile betting. If, however, the pot odds are 8/1 and the odds of your achieving a winning hand are 14/1, then it not worthwhile betting.

Calculating percentage chance of improving

To simplify the arithmetic, there is an easy calculation to make that is the approximate percentage chance of improving your hand. You first need to know how many cards can complete your hand (outs). You then double this number and add 2.

Example 1

With Texas hold 'em, if your pocket cards are two spades and the flop gives two spades, you have a chance of making a flush with spades. There are 13 spades in total. Four of them have been dealt, two to your hand and two to the flop. There are nine left in the deck (13 − 4 = 9).

This gives you nine outs: (9 x 2) + 2 = 20.

You therefore have approximately a 20 per cent chance of making the flush. Your bet should be no more than 20 per cent of the pot value. If there is £200 in the pot, for example, your bet should be less than £40 to be worthwhile.

Example 2

You have a pair of kings and want to calculate your chances of getting a third king. There are four kings, you have two, which leaves two in the deck. You therefore have two outs: (2 x 2) + 2 = 6.

You therefore have approximately a 6 per cent chance of making the three of a kind. Your bet should be no more than 6 per cent of the pot value. If there is £100 in the pot, your bet should be less than £6 to be worthwhile. If you need to bet, for example, £10 to stay in the game, it would be better to fold.

Effect of using wildcards

In some games, wildcards may be permitted. A wildcard is a card that can be used in place of any other card. If, for example, twos or jokers were wild, a two or a joker could be used to make up a higher ranking hand (see Figure 4.2).

The use of wildcards is common in private games. However, they drastically change the odds so you need to completely rethink the way you play the game.

Where wildcards are used, the higher ranking hands are much easier to achieve. Without wildcards, there are only four ways in which a royal flush can be made.

By having, for example twos wild, the number of ways a royal flush can be made hugely increases to 504. The odds of being dealt a royal flush are cut from 649,739/1 to 5156/1. All the other hands are also more easily achieved. What may have been a good hand in a game without wildcards may be a poor hand if wildcards are used.

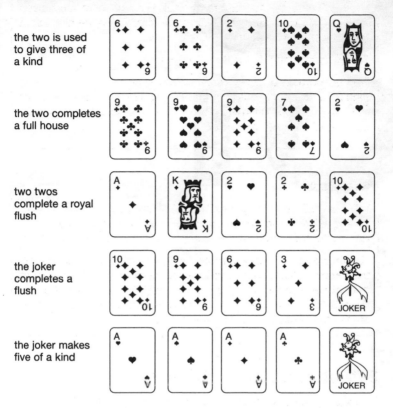

the two is used to give three of a kind

the two completes a full house

two twos complete a royal flush

the joker completes a flush

the joker makes five of a kind

figure 4.2 using wild cards

Instead of nominating one of the values already in use as wild, the jokers may be added to the pack and made wild. This will completely change the calculations again, as more cards are used. If one joker is added to the pack and made wild, the number of ways in which a royal flush can be made increases to 24. If three jokers are added, the number of possible five card poker hands increases to 3,478,761. The number of ways a royal flush can be made will be 224. The odds against a royal flush will be increased to 15,529/1.

05

betting

In this chapter you will learn:
- how to bet
- betting strategies
- what happens if a player runs out of money.

Betting terms

Ante

An ante is a bet that is made by all players before the cards are dealt. Each player bets an equal amount. The amount of the ante is agreed by the players. It is used as a means of increasing the pot to make the game more competitive. If, for example, there are eight players and there is an ante of £2, there is a minimum pot of £16 available to win. Without an ante, the players could simply fold with a mediocre hand. The ante gives players with a mediocre hand the incentive to stay in the game and try to win the pot. If a player is dealt a poor hand five times in a row, by this stage he has lost £10, even though his next hand is nothing special, he may decide to play it just to try to recoup his losses.

Blind bets

A blind bet is a bet that is made before the cards are seen. Some games like Texas hold 'em have players take it in turns to place a blind bet. The player who has placed the blind bet then has a greater incentive to play in order to win back the money he has contributed.

Check

Checking is not betting. This usually happens on the first round of betting after the cards have been dealt. Instead of betting a player announces 'check'. He does not contribute any money to the pot. If he wishes to continue in the game he must bet on his next turn. If all the players decide to check, new hands are dealt to everyone. Not all games allow players to check.

Some players will use checking as a strategy for hiding a good hand. They have a good hand but do not want to make it obvious on the first round of betting. This can, however, be a dangerous strategy as you run the risk that all the players check and your good hand is wasted.

Bet

Betting is making a bet. If you are the first player and you want to stay in the game, you bet at least the minimum bet. Supposing the minimum bet is £5; if you bet, you add £5 to the pot. In order to stay in the game, players must equal your bet.

Call

If a player announces call they simply match what was bet before. If the previous player bet £10, they must add £10 to the pot.

Fold

If a player does not want to bet, they fold. Their cards are returned to the dealer and placed in the muck pile. They take no further part in the game and can no longer win the pot.

Raise

A player may increase the bet by raising. They must match the previous bet and may raise up to the agreed limit. Suppose the previous bet was £5 and they raise by £5, they will contribute a total of £10 to the pot; £5 matches the previous bet and £5 is the raise. The next player must now contribute £10 to the pot to stay in the game. If a player raises, all the players must match the raise in order to stay in the game. A betting round continues until all players have called the last raise. When this happens, all remaining players have contributed the same amount to the pot. In the following example, each remaining player has contributed 10 chips to the pot.

Example		
Player	Action	Amount added to the pot
A	checks	0
B	bets 5	5
C	raises 5	10
D	folds	0
A	calls	10
B	calls	5

Fixed limit Texas hold 'em

In some games, there will be specified limits for betting, for example, £10/£20, where £10 is the amount of the bet in the early rounds of betting and £20 is the amount of the bets/raises in the later betting rounds.

Developing a betting strategy

You need to develop a betting strategy that will maximize your winnings while minimizing your losses. Your betting strategy also needs to be varied so that the other players can't predict your hand. If you always double the stakes when you have a good hand it will soon be noted by the other players. Players who always bet the minimum possible will immediately advertise their good hand if they suddenly place a huge bet.

From your player profiles you will have a good indication of your opponents' reactions to particular levels of betting. Some players may back down after a modest raise, while others may need a huge raise in order to fold. You will be able to spot the players who are staying in the game simply because it is not costing them very much. Your profile may tell you that one particular player always folds early on when he has nothing. If he is still there in the later round of betting, you will know to treat him with caution.

When to raise

Raising is used to force other players into folding and as a means of increasing the pot.

The way you bet throughout the game can determine whether you win or lose. See Figure 5.1. Suppose you are playing seven card stud. Your two hole cards (the cards that are dealt face down) are a pair of jacks (player A). The manner in which you bet early on could be enough to win you the game. If, after the third card is dealt, you make a big raise, you may force players to fold who could potentially beat you. After the first three cards, player B has a poor hand. He would be likely to fold if the stakes were suddenly increased.

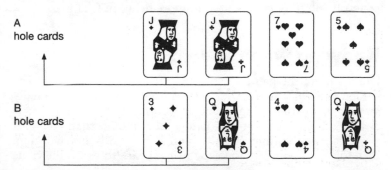

figure 5.1 betting strategy – knowing when to raise

However, the situation may be entirely different if you do not raise. Player B may continue playing, simply because it is not costing him very much. He still has the possibility of being dealt another queen. If his fourth card is a queen, he is then in a stronger position. If he then raises after this card, you arc in trouble, as you know you do not have enough to beat a pair of queens.

Another situation may arise if you have an exceptionally good hand such as a full house. You want to keep the other players betting for as long as possible to maximize the pot. Large bets early on will just increase the chance of everyone folding. If everyone folds, you only succeed in winning the ante. By placing smaller bets and gradually increasing them you can try to keep more players betting for longer. Your knowledge of the players will determine just how far you can raise the stakes without making them fold.

Bluffing

Just because your hand is poor it doesn't automatically mean you will lose. Having the nerve to bluff and back up the bluff with a heavy round of betting can cause other players to fold, even when their hands are better than yours. Do not expect to win every hand that you play. Bluffing should be used sparingly. If you bluff too often it can work against you. There will be situations where you have a fairly good hand but want to force out a players whom you suspect may have a slightly better hand. If you are known as a player who bluffs a lot, your strategy may not work. No matter how much you raise, your opponents will not back down. If, instead, you are known as a player who rarely bluffs, a large raise by you will be taken much more seriously. Bluffing is looked at in more detail in Chapter 6.

Knowing when to fold

Don't stay in the game for too long if your hand is poor. The earlier you fold the less money you will lose. By continually staying in for one extra round of betting with a hand that is clearly going to get beaten, you lose more money than you need to. If you are bluffing and the bluff is obviously not working, then fold. It is pointless to keep raising. Learn to assess the value of your hand early on. Appreciate the odds of converting it into a good hand. Analyse your opponents' likely hands. If you suspect their hand to be better than yours then fold.

Betting in casinos

Casinos will have written rules on how the betting is organized. You should get a copy of the rules and ensure that you understand them before betting.

Private games

Private games offer a great deal of flexibility as players can organize the betting in a wide range of ways. It is best to keep to a fairly simple method of betting. If you use a complicated system it can interfere with the game. You have enough to think about without having to perform complex calculations just to determine your next bet.

Whatever system you use, you should always agree a minimum and maximum bet and the amount of the ante.

Using a set limit

With this system, players agree both a minimum and a maximum bet. The range between the minimum and maximum should be fairly wide to give players the opportunity of making decent raises. If, for example, the gap between the minimum and maximum bet is only four chips, it does not give a player much opportunity to force other players to fold. Players will tend to stay in the game simply because it is not costing them very much. If you have a range of around 10 chips, a high raise will have more impact. Someone raising the stake by 10 chips will be able to force players into folding.

In the example that follows, an ante of one chip has been agreed, which means that each player must bet one chip before any cards are dealt. To stay in the game, each player must bet an amount equal to the previous player. They can also raise the stakes by betting an additional amount up to the maximum bet.

Minimum bet – 1 chip; maximum bet – 10 chips; ante – 1 chip
Four players – A, B, C and D

Player	Action taken	Stake	Total in pot
A, B, C and D	Ante	1 chip from each player	4
A	bets 2 chips	2	6
B	raises 2 chips	4	10
C	bets 4 chips	4	14
D	folds	0	14
A	raises 2 chips	6	20
B	raises 5 chips	11 *	31
C	folds	0	31
A	raises 2 chips	13	44
B	raises 10 chips	23 **	67
A	folds	0	67

Player B wins the pot of 67 chips. His stake was 39 chips.
Net winnings: 67 – 39 = 28 chips.

* Although the maximum bet is 10 chips, this is not the maximum number of chips that a player stakes. Player B's bet consists of a bet of 6 chips to match the previous bet, plus 5 chips, which is his own bet.
** Player B matches the previous bet of 13 chips and makes an additional bet of 10 chips.

table 5.1 example of betting using a set limit

Straddle method

In this method of betting, the first player makes a bet called the ante. The second player makes a bet that is double the ante, called the straddle. The cards, are dealt. After looking at his cards, the third player has two choices. He can either make a bet of double the straddle or withdraw from the game. The other players then take turns to decide whether or not to bet or withdraw from the game. To stay in the game, each player must bet at least the same amount as the previous player. Bets can also be increased, usually up to an agreed maximum. Betting will continue until no one else raises or the maximum bet is reached. The players then reveal their hands.

Ante – 2 chips; maximum bet – 20 chips; opening bet double last straddle

Four players – A, B, C and D

Player	Action	Stake	Total in pot
A	makes ante-bet	2 chips	2
B	doubles ante	4 chips	6
C	opens	8 chips	14
D	calls	8 chips	22
A	folds	0	22
B	raises 5	13 chips	35
C	calls	13 chips	48
D	folds	0	48
B	raises 10	23 chips	71
C	folds	0	71

Player B wins the pot of 71 chips. His stake was 40 chips.

Net winnings: 71 – 40 = 31 chips.

table 5.2 example of straddle method

No-limit Texas hold 'em betting

With Texas hold 'em, in the initial round of betting, the first player to bet makes a small blind bet and the second player makes a big blind. The subsequent players can then fold, call or raise. Their bet must be at least equal to the big blind and any raise at least equal to the previous bet or raise. The first two players have already contributed to the pot in the form of a small blind and big blind. When the betting reaches the small blind the amount that needs to be called is reduced by the amount of the small blind. If, for example, the previous bet was 1000 and the small blind was £100, then only 900 needs to be added to the pot to call.

Player	Options	Action taken	Amount added to pot
A	Must post small blind	Posts small blind	100
B	Must post big blind	Posts big blind	200
C	Fold, call 200, raise 200+	Raises 300	500
D	Fold, call 500, raise 300+	Raises 1000	1500
E	Fold, call 1500, raise 1000+	Calls	1500
F	Fold, call 1500, raise 1000+	Folds	0
A	Fold, call 1400, raise 1000+	Calls	1400
B	Fold, call 1300, raise 1000+	Calls	1300
C	Fold, call 1000 raise 1000+	Folds	0

table 5.3 example of no-limit Texas hold 'em betting

Freeze out

With this method of betting, each player has an equal amount of capital at the beginning of the game. The object is for one player to win all the chips. Betting is arranged using any agreed method. When a player runs out of chips, there is an immediate showdown and the player with the highest ranking hand wins the pot.

Pot-limit and no-limit games

In pot-limit games, the amount bet can be any amount up to the total value of the pot. In no-limit games, players can bet up to the value of their chips. Supposing they have £20,000 worth of chips, they could then place a bet for £20,000.

Running out of money

Occasionally a player may run out of money/chips midway through a game. In this situation, a second pot may be opened. The first pot is generally referred to as the main pot and the second pot is the sidepot. The remaining players make all further bets to the sidepot. The player with insufficient funds waits until either one player remains or there is a showdown. If one player remains, he wins the sidepot. His hand is then compared with that of the player who ran out of money. The player with the higher hand will win the main pot. If several players remain, a showdown will take place between these players and the one with the highest ranking hand wins the sidepot. That winning hand is then compared to that of the player who ran out of money. The player with the higher hand will win the main pot.

Occasionally, more than one player will go all in. In this situation, a new pot is created each time.

Example

There are three players A, B and C.

Player A bets 100
Player B bets all in 50
Player C calls 100

Two pots are created. The main pot will contain 150 chips – 50 from each player. The sidepot will contain 100 chips – the chips that A and C have contributed over and above what B has contributed.

There is a showdown between A and C for the sidepot. A's hand is A, A, 9, 5, 3. C's hand is 8, 8, 8, K, J. A has a pair of aces, C has three of a kind with eights and wins the sidepot.

There is then a showdown between C and B. B's hand is Q, Q, Q, 7, 2. B has three of a kind with queens and beats C's hand. B wins the main pot.

06

bluffing

In this chapter you will learn:
- when you should bluff
- how often to bluff
- how to spot other players bluffing.

What is bluffing?

If all the other players fold in a game of poker, the remaining player wins the pot and does not have to reveal the cards held to the other players. This means that it is possible to win a game without necessarily having the best hand. Bluffing is convincing the other players that you have a good hand when you actually have a poor hand. Bluffing is achieved by placing a big bet to intimidate the other players to fold. The advantage of bluffing is that it allows you to attempt to win a pot even when the cards that you have are poor in value and would have little chance of winning in a showdown. To succeed with a bluff you need to raise the betting to a level high enough to ensure that the players fold before the game reaches a showdown. If your bluff is successful you will win the pot and no one will know that you were bluffing. If, however, you are forced into a showdown, you must reveal your cards and your bluff will have failed.

Semi-bluffing

Semi-bluffing is making a big bet when your current hand is poor but has a good opportunity to improve. Your initial cards may not be enough to win a game but if you stay in until more cards are revealed you may get what you want to make a great hand. If you don't get the cards you want then you continue to play out the hand as if they are there. In Texas hold 'em, you may, for example, have two cards for a potential straight or flush. After the flop, you still need two cards to make a straight. You continue playing as if the flop had given you what you needed for a good hand. By sufficiently raising the stakes, you attempt to make the others fold. If this does not work, you continue to bet and hope that you get your necessary cards.

When should you bluff?

Bluffing can be used in most games of poker where you are competing against other players for a pot. This includes games such as five-card draw, seven-card stud, Texas hold 'em and Omaha. In games where you are playing against a casino dealer, like pai gow poker and Caribbean stud poker, you cannot bluff.

Bluffing does not work for all games. Bluffing is ineffective in low-stake games. Players will tend to stay in if it doesn't cost too much to continue playing. An extra chip or two when the chips are low in value will not make much difference to someone's bankroll.

Bluffing is most effective in high-stake games where it is possible to substantially increase bets. If it becomes expensive for a player to stay in a game, they are more likely to consider folding. Bluffing is particularly suited to no-limit texas hold 'em, because you can bet what you like: you can make a huge bet that is big enough to make anyone think twice before continuing to play.

The size of the pot will influence your decision on whether or not to bluff. Bluffing is most useful for taking small pots. In a situation where lots of players have folded, you are left with little competition for the pot. With a small pot, players are more likely to fold if they have a mediocre hand. Although they could improve, they will often prefer to sit the game out and wait for a better hand with a bigger pot. In contrast, a large pot will be much more competitive. Players will be more likely to fight for a pot to which they have contributed a substantial stake.

Tournaments offer more opportunities for bluffing than normal games. This is because players tend to play tightly taking few risks. Play is against strangers and in the initial stages the players will want to assess their opponents. As play progresses and players get short on chips, they will want to save them for their best hands and not risk getting involved in a high round of betting that could cost them the tournament.

If you play with a regular group of players, knowing your opponents is important. You will also have an idea of the sort of hand that a particular opponent plays. Do they tend to wait for really good hands before playing or will they go with a mediocre hand and hope to improve? You will need to learn what makes them fold and what doesn't. Some players will never fold and will always stay in until the conclusion of a game. If up against such a player you will always be involved in a showdown and, if their cards are better, you will be beaten. The other players will also see that you have been trying to bluff, which will affect your credibility as a tight player. It is therefore pointless bluffing in this situation.

If you are playing with weak players it is not worthwhile bluffing. They are less likely to recognize that you are trying to convince them that you have a good hand. They will tend to just keep betting to stay in the game. In weak games, you may also come across players who bluff practically all the time and will keep playing to a showdown.

Bluffing is best used against good players. A good player will realize that your increase in stakes means that you either have a good hand or that you are bluffing. If you have a reputation as a tight player, the increase in stakes will be taken seriously.

Bluffing will not always work. Not every player will back down, particularly if they believe that they have a good hand. If you find yourself in the situation where your bluff is not believed, it may be better to fold earlier rather than later. If you are continually re-raised, you can quickly lose all your chips.

Ideally, you should bluff when there are just a few people left in the game. It is easier to convince one or two people that you have a good hand rather than having to convince five or six.

Your position in relation to the dealer will have an influence on whether or not it is worthwhile to bluff. It is not good to bluff from an early position as you have no idea if the other players have been dealt a good hand or not. It is much better to bluff from a late position as you will see the players' reactions to their hands and how they bet. If everyone has checked, this shows that their hands are not particularly special. It is easier to bluff when players show weakness by checking on a previous round compared to showing strength by betting. Making a big bet can show that you have a good hand when you have nothing. With Texas hold 'em, the only two unknowns are the two blinds. Depending on how they bet will determine whether or not to continue with a bluff or fold. A strong raise from one of the blinds could indicate that they have a good hand. It could equally indicate that they, too, are trying to bluff. You will have to use your knowledge of the players to decide your next move. If everyone folds on the first round of betting and you are left with just the two blinds, then most of the competition has been eliminated. By betting, you could convince the blinds that you have a decent hand.

A good time to bluff is when you have just won a big pot with a good hand. A forceful round of betting will be more likely to convince the other players that your luck is in and you've got another good hand.

It's important not to get caught bluffing, as this will lose you credibility. You need to be able to force players to fold without getting caught in a showdown. If you've recently been caught bluffing, players will tend to call your bets. You can, however, use getting caught to your advantage, if shortly after you have a good hand. The other players will remember that you just bluffed and are more likely to assume that you are trying to pull off another bluff. You can then use this opportunity to raise your stakes and take a big pot.

You should bluff when other players are running short on chips. They are more likely to fold in order to play in the next game. You will need to take care if they stay in, however, as if they go all in, you will be forced to a showdown. Avoid bluffing against players with lots of chips as they are more likely to carry on betting.

Bluffs that seem to present a specific hand like a flush, straight or full house have a much better chance of success. Trying to convince the other players that you have made a good hand will be easier. If there appears to be nothing on the board, it will be harder to convince the other players that you have anything special.

A bluff when you are on a losing streak or when you are low on chips comes across as desperation and is less likely to be believed by the other players. If you have to go all in, you will be forced to a showdown and your bluff will be revealed, which will reduce your credibility.

Your knowledge of the other players will be a help. If you are up against players who tend to fold easily then you can pull off a bluff.

With Texas hold 'em, be wary of bluffing when there are high cards in the flop like A, K, Q, J or 10, as someone will inevitably have a match and will be highly unlikely to back down. If there is an ace in the flop, there is bound to be someone who already has an ace in their hand.

For example, with a flop of A, K, J anyone holding an ace, king or jack will stay in, anyone with a pair of aces, pair of kings or pair of jacks will stay in. So, too, will anyone holding a queen with the hope of getting a straight. The competition for the pot will be too great. If the board ends up as A, K, J, 10, 7, anyone with a queen, knows that they have nuts. Anyone with three of a kind will likely stay in. Anyone with an ace and another high card may also stay in. Those who have just missed their hand may also stay in and attempt a bluff.

If there are low cards in the flop, it is less likely that someone will have a match. Players are much more likely to stay in with high cards. If you start betting strongly as if you have a three of a kind or a high pair, this is more likely to be believed. You need to ensure that you bet strongly enough to force out your opponents before more cards are dealt.

If you bet pre-flop and didn't get the desired hand after the flop, continue betting as if you got what you wanted. The players will note your strong position pre-flop and your apparently stronger position post-flop.

Keep an eye on the players who have folded; they will inevitably show that they threw away a good hand. If they had a matching pair in their hand, then it diminishes the chances that the other players have a good hand.

In five card draw, it is a common bluff to take just two cards on the draw in an attempt to let the other players think that you already have a possible three of a kind rather than just a pair and a kicker. To make the bluff pay off, you need to back it up with a high bet.

How often should you bluff?

Every game is different and you will have to learn to judge when it is an opportune moment to bluff. Bluffing should be used sparingly. Having a good hand is more likely to win you a game than a bluff. As a rule of thumb, a bluff should be used no more than once every 20 to 30 hands.

If you watch televised poker, it may appear that bluffing is commonplace. This is due to the television companies tending to show the most exciting highlights and someone trying to pull off a bluff is more interesting to watch than an average, no-bluffing game.

Getting caught bluffing once in a while will not have a negative effect; however, it is not good to get a reputation as a bluffer. If you constantly bluff, the other players will not be convinced when you raise the stakes and will tend to take you all the way to a showdown.

It is much better to develop the image of a tight player who only bets with a good hand and folds with a poor hand. If you then go with a bluff, you are more likely to convince the other players that you have a good hand. The other players will be wary of your raising stakes as you have a reputation for only going with the best hands.

Spotting when other players are bluffing

You will need to assess whether or not another player is bluffing or has a good hand. The sort of questions you need to ask yourself in order to weigh up the situation are:

Is the player taking advantage of a late position?

Is the pot small?

Are there just a few players left?

Has everyone else checked?

Does the player's body language tell you anything?

Is the player a known bluffer?

Is the player on a losing streak?

Is the player taking advantage of a recent, big win?

07

body language

In this chapter you will learn:
- about body language
- how to spot a tell
- about signs of bluffing.

To play poker well you need to discern what sort of hand the other players have got in order to decide whether or not your hand is worth playing. The way that a person conducts themselves in a game can give you some clues to help you make a decision. Everyone has habits, ways of behaving and physical reactions that are difficult to control. Learning to recognize these can help you to work out if a player really has a good hand or if they are bluffing. The way that an individual reacts will be personal to them, so you may see different responses to the same situation in different people.

What is a tell?

In poker if a player always responds in the same way to a certain situation this is called a tell. A tell is a physical sign that gives away the hand that someone is holding. It will be a particular habit that shows when the player has a good or a bad hand. It can be the way the player bets. They may have a set betting pattern depending on how good their hand is. If they get a good hand they bet in a certain way. If they bluff they bet in a different way. It can be the way a player sits at the table, a scratch of the head, a nervous tic, a cough – almost any physical mannerism.

Looking for tells is an aid to help you discern what a player's hand is, although using a tell to win a hand should be no substitute for good play. You are more likely to win with good hands – but spotting a tell will give you a slight edge.

Bluffing and lying

When someone bluffs in poker they are basically lying about their hand. When people lie, there are a number of classic signs they may demonstrate. Some people are better liars than others and can easily disguise their deception. For this reason, you will have to carefully observe your opponents and try to find out if they have any mannerisms that give them away. If a player is caught bluffing, take note of what made the bluff obvious. You may be able to use this knowledge to catch the player bluffing in a future game.

Some classic signs of lying are bringing the hand up to the face, covering the mouth, stroking the chin, playing with the hair and crossing the arms. There are liars who will do none of these and there are those people who will do all some or just a few of them.

Some people tend to look down when lying. A quick glance to the upper right can be a sign of lying. Others will maintain eye contact to convince you that they are being truthful.

The most obvious sign that a poker player is lying is a change in behaviour. If a player is suddenly sitting very still and quiet when they were previously moving in a relaxed manner then you need to be suspicious. If a player who was previously quiet and relaxed is behaving as if they have a lousy hand or acting like they've got a great hand you should take note. Does a player project a natural air of confidence? Is a player obviously nervous?

Tells to look for

Anxiety

The advantage that you have in poker is that money is at stake. This puts the players under stress and they are more likely to show signs of anxiety if they play a poor hand. When we are anxious, the body has problems remaining still. This may produce reactions like the flexing of muscles, eye pupil dilation, heart palpitations and a dry throat.

Things to look out for are:

fidgeting – the player can't sit still and keeps changing position in their seat; nervous movement of the feet or legs; the player starts fiddling with chips, smokes more than usual or has trembling hands

a change of voice, including the pitch or stuttering

taking more sips of a drink

sweating

changes in the vein on the top side of face shows a fluctuation in blood pressure

licking the lips

handling objects

asking questions about your hand.

Acting

Some players will start acting to give the impression that their hand is good when it is really bad and vice versa. Try to look at the player's initial reaction to their hand. A smile that is quickly replaced by a frown as the player remembers to act can tell you that the player has something good. An initial frown followed by a smile can tell you that the player has a bad hand. A player who tries to pretend that they have a lousy hand and is staying in just for fun may try too hard to convince you of their bad hand. The same too applies to a bluffer who may appear too overconfident in a hand.

There are distinct differences between real expressions and feigned expressions. The face can make 5000 expressions so it can be deduced from this whether or not someone is lying. Poker players will try to show a neutral expression – the classic poker face. There are some clues that you can look for. A fake smile will give no movement of the wrinkle lines around the eyes. Many people assume that a liar will tend to avoid eye contact but a good liar is just as likely to look you directly in the eye. Some people will blink more when lying and others will blink less. To hide their facial expressions some poker players wear sunglasses, a cap or visor.

Stance

The way that a player sits at the table can give away a hand. A player who slumps shows a lack of confidence and is likely to have a bad hand. A player who sits up straight when they get their cards shows that they have something good and they are getting ready to act. Increased leaning forward can be a sign that the player is bluffing.

Looking at cards

The length and number of times that a player looks at their cards can give you information. A player who constantly looks at their hand is likely to have a good hand. A player with a good hand may continually go back to look at the cards.

In Texas hold 'em, a player who looks at their hand after the flop may be trying to work out if they're in with a chance of making a flush or a straight.

Keep an eye on players who have folded. They will often give away information. In Texas hold 'em their reaction to the flop may indicate that they threw away a good hand that matched with their cards. If you can discern this, you will know that the chances of the other players getting a match are diminished.

How a player speaks can give you some clues about their hands. Liars will tend to repeat questions to give them more time to compile an answer. If you ask someone, 'Have you got a good hand?' and they reply, 'Have I got a good hand?' chances are they don't. Liars also tend to avoid contractions. They will say 'I do not' rather than 'I don't'. Some players will ask questions about your hand to try to get some clues. They will watch how you respond to see if you give anything away.

Betting

Look for repetitive betting patterns. A player may advertise their hand by always betting the same way with a good hand. They may bet a particular way with a mediocre hand and bet yet another way when bluffing.

Also assess how long it takes the players to bet. Someone who has already decided to bluff may have worked out that they are going to bet in this round regardless of what happens. They may have their chips ready to put in the pot before it is their turn to act. Someone who is considering bluffing may take a little time to come to a decision. With Texas hold 'em, someone with a good hand will have decided that they want to bet through to the flop and will bet confidently. Someone with a mediocre hand may take time to weigh up whether or not they should bet or fold. They may hesitate and look at their stack deciding whether or not to bet. Hesitation can also be an act. If it goes on too long, it's probably a player with a good hand feigning weakness.

Controlling your body language

A survey by bookmaking firm Victor Chandler found that 58 per cent of poker players are looking for tells. This means that most of your opponents will be carefully watching your behaviour. In order to not give away information about your hand, you will need to make sure that you don't have any tells. If you do get caught bluffing, ask the other players how they knew it was a bluff. You may get told outright that you gave it away by fidgeting or frowning or with some other mannerism. If you are aware of your behaviour you can modify it to disguise it.

Avoid acting to give out false messages about your hand. Most people are bad actors.

Sit still at the table.

Avoid fidgeting, playing with chips or touching your face.

Try to stay relaxed.

Sit up straight.

Look at your cards just once and remember them.

Quickly decide how good your hand is, what will threaten it and how you are going to play it.

Bet confidently without hesitation.

Assessing the competition

If you play against strangers, you probably won't be playing with them for long enough to spot tells. If you play with a regular crowd, you will have longer to study your opponents and may notice something about their behaviour which is typical to them in a particular situation. With Texas hold 'em, for example, they may get into the habit of always raising pre-flop when they are bluffing. They may be eager to bet without hesitation when they bluff. Not everyone will have a tell but if you can pick out one or two players that do, you will manage to reduce the competition for the pot.

If you play with regular players, keep a diary of their habits. It may take you a few sessions to spot anything that can be useful. You may notice, for example, that a particular player always starts playing with their chips when they are bluffing or another puts on an act to feign a poor hand when they actually have a good hand. Before play read through your diary to refresh your mind.

If you discover a tell, never reveal it to the other players. Once you know a player's weakness you can continue to profit from it. If you reveal it to the other players, they can also exploit it. Never tell the player himself as he may modify his behaviour.

Type of player

You can divide up players into different classes. Each type of player has a different way of reacting.

A strong, experienced player will give very little away. They will likely be expressionless and move little. Against these players you need to concentrate on playing good hands and making sure you don't give out any signals about your own hand.

Aggressive players will try to intimidate you. They may attack with big bets, stare you in the eye or ask you questions about your hand. All these tactics are used to make you fold rather than play. You need to learn to ignore these aggressive tactics and just play your hand. If you have a good hand worth playing, don't be scared off.

Novice players are still learning and will make all kinds of mistakes. They may play a hand confidently in the wrong belief that it is a good hand. They are more likely to overact and feign the opposite hand to the one they actually have. They will try too hard to let you believe that they have a poor hand when they actually have a good hand. They will also take their time to decide what to do.

Online poker

Online poker presents an entirely different challenge. You can't see the players, so it is difficult to find tells. However, there are some indications that can give you a clue. Someone who checks very quickly may have a weak hand. With Texas hold 'em, a fast bet on the turn or on the river can indicate a strong hand. A player who is slow to respond is likely to have a weak hand. A player who hesitates then checks is likely to have a weak hand. Hesitation followed by a raise shows strength. Using automatic play means that the player will have a set pattern of play. If the play suddenly changes, this probably means that the player has a good hand or is attempting a bluff.

08
cheating

In this chapter you will learn:
- how players cheat
- how to combat cheating
- about shuffling the cards.

Poker is particularly vulnerable to cheating. There are lots of ways in which players can be duped. Playing in legal casinos is the safest way to ensure that the games are played fairly. If you play in private games, you should be aware of the many methods of cheating so that you can ensure that you are not conned. If you suspect other players of cheating, you should stop playing.

Holding cards

This is where a player steals a card from the deck, usually an ace, and keeps it up a sleeve or on their lap until it is needed for a hand. The cheat will usually acquire the card from a hand that is folded. Instead of putting all folded cards in the muck pile, they will keep one. It is then switched into play when it gets matched. If you suspect this form of cheating, you can check for held cards by counting the number of cards in the deck. Since the aces are the most desired cards, a quicker method is to check that all the aces are in the deck. Before shuffling and dealing, you fan out all the cards face up on the table. It takes barely a couple of seconds to make sure all the aces are present.

Reflective surfaces

Obviously you should not play in rooms with mirrors, but other reflective surfaces can allow a cheat to find out what cards players are holding. Check the light fittings as some glass lampshades act as excellent mirrors. With the correct lighting, it is very easy to see what cards are being dealt to players if a table has a highly polished glass or marble surface. You should always, therefore, play on a table covered in felt or a cloth.

Make sure that there is nothing on the table that can act as a mirror, like a metal lighter or glass ashtray. The dealer only needs to pass the cards over the top of a shiny object as they are dealt to see their value. Clear the table of all unnecessary items.

If you wear glasses, be aware that they can act as mirrors, showing the other players your hand. If you hold your cards up to your face, your glasses may be reflecting your hand to everyone else at the table.

Betting light

One of the easiest ways to cheat is for players not to contribute fully to the pot. If there are a lot of chips already in the pot, it is not always obvious how many chips a particular player is adding. You may see him pick up the required number of chips, but it is very easy to just drop a few into the pot and palm the rest. Everyone's attention then switches to the next player and the one who palmed the chips is able to discreetly put them back on the table with his own chips.

Alternatively, a cheat may bet so quickly that you do not see what chips he picks up. The only indication that you get of a bet being made is the clinking of chips as more are added.

Marked cards

In poker, it is advantageous for players to know what cards the other players are holding. Anyone with this knowledge is able to bet only when he knows he has a winning hand.

The easiest way to accomplish this is to mark the backs of the cards in such a way so that they can be 'read' by the cheat. The designs on the backs of the cards are often intricate patterns. It is possible to add shading, small dots or to slightly thicken lines. These changes will not be noticed by the other players unless the cards are carefully scrutinized.

Even if someone produces a sealed pack of cards, they may still be marked. It is a relatively simple task to mark the cards and reseal them in their original packaging. Professionally marked cards can also be purchased. The designs may be identical but certain cards may have a slightly thicker border on one side.

Before you begin playing you should carefully study the cards. Pay particular attention to the corners. Marks are placed here so that they can be seen when players are holding their cards. Compare the high cards with the low cards. Often only the high cards will be marked.

It is also easy to mark the cards when they are in play. When a cheat gets, for example, an ace in their hand, they may crease the corner so that they can recognize it in other players hands in subsequent games. Alternatively, a small indentation in the corner of a card will be made with a fingernail. It is less obvious than a crease but is visible enough to a cheat.

Cards should be checked before and during the course of play as they can become marked either intentionally or accidentally. If any marks are found, use a new deck of cards.

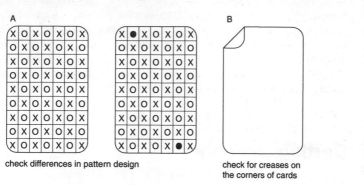

A

check differences in pattern design

B

check for creases on the corners of cards

figure 8.1 cheating using marked cards

Technicians

Dealers can cheat in lots of ways. Someone who is skilled at manipulating the cards is called a technician. It is easy to look at the bottom card while shuffling. With practice, it is possible to position desired cards at the bottom of the pack. The dealer can then deal his hand from the bottom of the deck and the other players' hands from the top.

Another method is to spot a good card while shuffling and to place it on the top of the deck. The dealer saves this card for himself and deals from the second card down to the other players.

A player can also use a spiked ring to make an indentation in the cards. When it is his turn to deal, he simply has to feel the cards to identify the best ones. He can either save them for himself using one of the techniques already described or simply keep track of which player receives them.

Dealing extra cards

A dealer can give himself an advantage by dealing an extra card to his hand. A dealer can also collude with another player and give his partner additional cards. The cheat then simply discards the lowest value card. The extra card may just get dropped on the floor or hidden in a pocket. If you find a low-value card on the floor after a game then it is likely that someone has used this method.

Five-card draw is vulnerable to cheating with extra cards. A player can simply call out that he is exchanging three cards and only put one or two on the muck pile. This way he gets an extra card and simply disposes of the lowest value card. To counteract this, players should separate the cards that they wish to discard and fan them out on the table to show that they are discarding the correct number.

Cutting the cards

To combat cheating by the dealer it is common practice for one of the players to cut the cards. However, the dealer can overcome the problem of the cards being cut by bending one card in the middle so that it is slightly curved. The cards will tend to be cut at the curved card. Try this yourself with a pack of cards – you will find that you easily grip the curved card but the ones below it slip through your fingers. A dealer cannot guarantee that it will work every time but on the occasions when it does, he is guaranteed of a win.

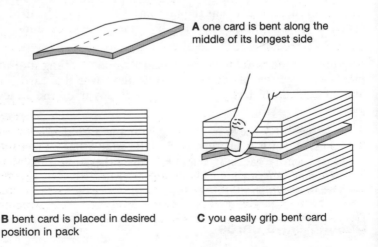

A one card is bent along the middle of its longest side

B bent card is placed in desired position in pack

C you easily grip bent card

figure 8.2 how a cheat can ensure cards cut in a certain place

Some players will just tap the top of the cards to show that they do not want to cut them. This should be discouraged as it makes it easy for a dealer to cheat.

Sometimes a cut will take place but the dealer will reverse the cut. This can be achieved in a number of ways with sleight of hand.

Stealing

Watch out for players stealing chips from the pot. It is easy to give the appearance that you are adding chips to the pot when you are actually taking them.

Keep an eye on players who help you to collect your winnings. It is easy for someone to palm a high-value chip and then add it to one of their stacks. Also be wary of distractions – it is then very easy for players to steal from the pot or to steal chips from other players.

Collusion

Poker relies on players not knowing each other's hands. If two or more people are colluding, they can ensure that their best hand is always played. The colluding players will have a set of signals to tell the other player their hand. This could be anything from the position of their fingers, the way the chips are placed, the lighting of a cigarette or the scratching of an ear. The players may simply quickly flash their cards to each other.

The player with the poorer hand will simply drop out of the betting, letting the one with the better hand continue to play. They will not beat your hand every time but they will do so enough to give them an edge. You could even be in a situation where an entire team is colluding. Everyone at the table is working together against you. It appears to be a normal game as different people win different games. They may even let you win a few pots to give you confidence. However, their ultimate goal is to win your entire bankroll. They simply share the profits between themselves.

Cold deck

A cold deck is a deck of cards that has been arranged in a preset order that will give the dealer or another colluding player the winning hand. The cold deck is prepared before the game and kept hidden in a player's pocket. The cold deck can be brought into play by the dealer or another player who, using sleight of hand or a distraction, will switch decks.

The cheat may prepare the deck so that, for example, he gets a full house. Other players may also be dealt good hands, such as three of a kind or a straight. The other players will then bet heavily, confident that they have really good hands. This will help to maximize the pot. Knowing that he has the best hand, the cheat only has to continue on to the showdown to take a big pot.

False calling of a hand

This can happen at a showdown. A player with a straight with all black cards may declare a straight flush and quickly clear away the cards before the other players have a chance to notice the error. If you are involved in a showdown, you should carefully scrutinize the other player's cards to ensure that they have really beaten your hand.

Modern technology

Modern technology is providing cheats with new ways to fix games. Cameras have become smaller and therefore easier to conceal. Their images can be transmitted wirelessly. Cheats have been caught using fibre-optic cables in casinos to see cards being dealt. The pictures get sent to an accomplice who communicates the hands of the other players to the cheat via an earpiece. These scams invariably get detected in casinos, but private games are more susceptible.

Combating cheating

If you play in private games, be particularly wary of playing cards with strangers. A group of cheats working together can easily make a game look like it is legitimate when their only purpose is to take your bankroll.

Always play with new, sealed decks of cards. Check that the box has not been previously opened and resealed. Check that the cellophane is intact. Count the cards before playing to check that the aces haven't been removed and are sitting up someone's sleeve. To be certain that the aces are there, fan the cards out face up.

Always insist on checking the cards for marks before and after play. Watch the dealer carefully. Does he hold the cards in an unusual way? Someone dealing the second or bottom card is likely to cover the cards with his hands. Always cut the cards by inserting a card not in play, like a joker. This gets round the problem of someone bending one of the cards. Insist that the cards are always cut before dealing. Do not allow players the option of not cutting the cards. Keep track of how much money goes into the pot. Carefully watch other players when they make their bets. Make sure they add the correct number of chips required. Make it a rule that only the winner may touch the winning pot.

Insist that players keep their hands above the table at all times during the game. If a player wants to get something from his pocket, like a handkerchief, during the game make it a rule that the player must clear his hands before and after doing so. The player simply does what dealers do in a casino; they show their hands palms up, so that everyone can see that they are empty. You can make it a rule that if, during a game, a player puts his hands under the table or in his pockets, his hand is declared dead.

If you suspect other players of cheating, stop playing.

Burning of cards

Another way to try to combat cheating by the dealer is for several cards to be 'burnt. After the cards have been shuffled and cut, the top five cards of a deck are removed and not used in play. However, a skilled technician can still shuffle the cards in such a say that his desired hand will be achieved.

Ensuring fair play

To ensure fair play it is best to play poker in legal casinos. Here, new cards are used each day and they are checked for marks before and after use. If cards do become marked during the course of play, they will be exchanged for new cards. The dealer controls all the betting and will ensure that the players contribute the correct number of chips. Cameras are installed on all the tables to record the actions, so if you suspect either a player or the dealer of cheating, there is a record of the game, which can be studied. If a cheat is caught, he will be barred from the casino and his details will be passed to other casinos. He may also face prosecution.

Shuffling and dealing the cards

The overhand style of shuffling where a number of cards are picked up from the back of the pack and dropped, a few cards at a time, to the front of the pack, is most open to abuse. The dealer can easily look at the faces of cards while they are being shuffled and arrange them into virtually any desired order.

To ensure the cards are really well mixed, it is best to use a combination of methods for shuffling. Laying the cards face down the table and giving them a good mix is a good method of shuffling. This should be combined with a riffle shuffle. Here, the pack is split into two and your thumbs are used to riffle the cards so that the two halves are combined (see Figure 8.3). The riffle shuffle can still be open to abuse as a dealer can ensure that some of the top few cards or some of the bottom do not get shuffled. So, after shuffling the cards should always cut by a player other than the dealer.

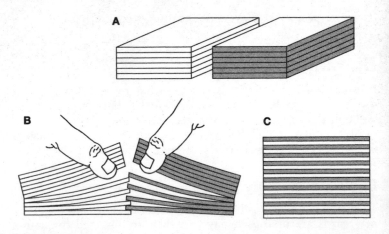

figure 8.3 the riffle shuffle

To eliminate cheating by the dealer, a card shoe can be used to hold the cards while dealing. This stops a dealer from dealing from the bottom of the deck or dealing the second card in a deck.

It is very important that players do not see either the card on the bottom of the pack or any discarded cards. If a player does see other cards he can use that information to his advantage. Suppose you see that the card on the bottom of the pack is a king. If you are dealt a pair of queens, you already know that the odds of being beaten by a pair of kings is reduced.

Ensure that none of the cards is exposed when you deal. Make it a rule that exposed cards are dead and are automatically shuffled. Take particular care that the bottom card cannot be seen by any of the players. Angle the cards down towards the table when you deal. Burn the top five cards. Take care not to reveal cards that have been discarded.

09

different games of poker

In this chapter you will learn:
- how to play different games
- how the betting is organized.

Five-card draw

Before the cards are dealt, each player makes an ante-bet.

Each player receives five cards face down. The players look at their cards. A betting round follows starting from the left of the dealer and proceeding clockwise.

Players have the option of checking, calling, raising or folding.

Betting continues until everyone either folds or calls after a raise or initial bet.

After the first round of betting is completed, each player may replace from none to five cards in their hand.

The player must decide which cards to discard before receiving new ones. Discarded cards are placed face down on the table apart from the cards retained.

New cards are dealt from the deck to replace the discarded cards. If, for example, you discard two cards, you will receive two new cards from the deck. The hand that you have now been dealt is the one that counts in a showdown.

A second betting round follows.

If no one raises, a showdown takes place.

If a player raises, betting continues until all remaining players call. If all the remaining players call, a showdown takes place.

If no one calls the final bet, the player making the final bet wins the pot and does not have to show his hand.

Any players still left proceed to a showdown.

The highest hand wins.

After an initial round of betting you have the opportunity to exchange any card in your hand. Hands are ranked according to the standard ranking of hands (see page 23).

Example

There are five players A, B, C, D, and E

Player A is the dealer

The ante – each puts £1 into the pot

The deal – each player receives five cards

First betting round – B bets £1, C calls (puts £1 in the pot), D folds, E raises £1 (puts £2 in the pot), A folds, B calls (£2), C calls (£2).

Discard – B discards three cards, C discards two, E discards one.

Second deal – B receives three cards, C receives two cards, E receives one card.

Second betting round – B bets £2, C folds, E raises £2 (£4), B raises £2 (£6), E calls (£6).

Showdown – B has K, K, 7, 5, 3 (one pair), E has 8, 8, 7, 7, 3 (two pair).

E wins the pot.

Five-card stud

Each player makes an ante-bet.

Each player receives one card face down (hole card) and one card face up (door card).

The player with the lowest face up card makes the first bet.

The first betting round takes place.

Each player is dealt a third card face up (third street).

The second betting round takes place.

Each player is dealt a fourth card face up (forth street).

The third betting round takes place.

Each player is dealt a fifth and final card face up (river).

The last betting round takes place followed by the showdown.

In the first round of betting, the player with the lowest face-up card bets first with a bet equivalent to half the lower limit. Suits are ranked spades highest, then hearts, diamonds, clubs.

In subsequent betting rounds, the highest hand bets first. If hands are tied, the player with the highest hand who is first to the left of the dealer bets first.

The first two rounds of betting are at the lower stake level and the last two rounds are at the higher stake level. So in a £1/£2 game, bets and raises are £1 in the first two rounds and £2 in the last two rounds.

Example

Stakes £2/£4

There are five players A, B, C, D and E

Player A is the dealer

Ante – each player contributes £1 to the pot

The first two cards are dealt, one face down, one face up

The face-up cards are: A – J, B – 10, C – 7, D – 2, E – K

D has the lowest card so must bet £1

First betting round – E calls (£2), A calls (£2), B calls (£2), C folds, D folds.

A third card is dealt. The face-up cards are: A – J, J, B – 10, 8, E – K, 10.

Second betting round – A is showing the highest hand so bets first. A bets £2, B folds, E raises £2 (£4), A calls.

A fourth card is dealt. The face-up cards are: A – J, J, 9, E – K, 10, J.

Third betting round – A is showing the highest hand so bets first. A bets £4, E raises £4 (£8), A calls.

A fifth card is dealt: A – J, J, 9, 7, E – K, 10, J , 6.

Fourth betting round – A is showing the highest hand so bets first. A bets £4, E raises £4 (£8), A raises £4 (£12), E calls.

Showdown – A has J, J, J, 9, 7 (three of a kind), B has K, K, 10, J, 6 (a pair of kings).

A wins.

Seven-card stud

Each player receives seven cards. The aim is to make the best possible five-card poker hand from the seven cards. The player with the best hand wins the pot.

Each player contributes an ante to the pot. The ante is agreed by the players. Three cards are dealt: two face down (hole cards), one face up (door card). The first round of betting takes place. The player with the lowest face-up card bets first. This first bet is equivalent to half of the lower stake. If two players each have the lowest card, the one with the lowest ranking suit bets first. Clubs is lowest followed by diamonds, hearts then spades. If, for example, two players both have the lowest card with a value of three, one with the three of diamonds and one with the three of spades, the player with the three of diamonds will bet first. Following bets are equal to the lower stake, so in a £1/£2 game, the bet will be £1. Each player may make a maximum of four bets in each betting round.

A fourth card (fourth street) is dealt face up, followed by the second round of betting. The player with the highest ranking hand showing bets first. Bets are at the lower stake level. A fifth card (fifth street) is dealt face up, followed by the third round of betting. Bets are at the higher stake level. A sixth card (sixth street) is dealt face up, followed by the fourth round of betting. Bets are at the higher stake level. So in a £1/£2 game, the bets are £2. The seventh and final card (river) is dealt face down, followed by the last round of betting. The showdown then takes place. The player who bet first on the final round of betting must show their cards first. If the other players have lower hands they do not have to show their cards. The player with the highest ranking five-card hand wins.

Summary

Ante

Two cards dealt face down and one face up

First betting round

Fourth card dealt face up (fourth street)

Second betting round

Fifth card dealt face up (fifth street)

Third betting round

Sixth card dealt face up (sixth street)

Fourth betting round
Seventh card dealt face down (river)
Final betting round
Showdown

Example

£5/£10, ante £1
There are five players A, B, C, D and E
Ante – each player contributes £1 to the pot

The first three cards are dealt and the players are showing the following:

A has 8
B has ace
C has 7
D has Q
E has 9

First betting round – C has the lowest card so bets first (£2.50), D calls, E calls, A calls, B calls.

The fourth card is dealt:

A has 8, 4
B has ace, 3
C has 7, J
D has Q, J
E has 9, 5

Second betting round – B has the highest ranking hand showing so bets first (£5), C calls, D calls, E calls, A folds.

The fifth card is dealt:

B has ace, 3, 6
C has 7, J, 9
D has Q, J, Q
E has 9, 5, K

Third betting round – D has the highest ranking hand showing so bets first (£10). E folds, B calls, C calls.

The sixth card is dealt:

B has ace, 3, 6, 2
C has 7, J, 9, 5
D has Q, J, Q, 3

Fourth betting round – D has the highest ranking hand showing so bets first (£10). B calls, C calls.

The seventh card is dealt:

B has ace, 3, 6, 2, K
C has 7, J, 9, 5
D has Q, J, Q, 3

Final betting round – D has the highest ranking hand showing so bets first (£10). B raises £10 (£20). C calls, D folds.

B's cards are ace, ace, ace, 3, 6, 2, K – his best hand is A, A, A, K, 6 – three of a kind with aces.

C has 10, 8, 7, J, 9, 5 – his best hand is J, 10, 9, 8, 7 – a straight.

C wins.

Texas hold 'em

Each player receives two cards face down. Five cards are then placed face up in the centre of the table and these cards are used by all the players. Each player uses any combination of the two cards in his hand and the five community cards to make the best five-card poker hand.

The deal

Initially, each player receives his two hidden cards followed by a round of betting. The player to the left of the dealer makes the first bet called the small blind, the next player makes the next bet called the big blind. Subsequent players then have the option of calling, raising or folding.

Their action will be based on how good they judge their two hidden cards to be. The next three cards are dealt, this is called the flop. These are community cards and are placed face up on the table. Players look at these cards and judge the possible hand that could be made by the end of the game using these cards and their cards. This is followed by another round of betting. A fourth community card is dealt followed by a round of betting. Then the last community card is dealt, followed by a round of betting. The first two rounds of betting are at the lower limit and the last two rounds of betting are at the higher limit. Any remaining players then take part in a showdown. The highest ranking hand wins the pot.

Summary

Blind bets placed

Initial deal – two cards face down to each player

First betting round

The flop – three community cards are dealt

Second betting round

The turn – a fourth community card is dealt

Third betting round

The river – the fifth community card is dealt

Final betting round

Showdown

Split pots

Split pots are common in Texas hold 'em. A split pot occurs when both players have the same ranking hand. Suppose player A has Q, J and player B has ace, Q. The board is J, 10, 9, 8, 3:

A has Q, J, 10, 9, 8
B has Q, J, 10, 9, 8

It is a common misconception with split pots that if both players have the same ranking hand, the player with the highest pocket cards (the player's two cards) wins. This is not true. Only the five cards that make the winning hand count. All other cards are irrelevant. In this case, the fact that player B also has an ace is irrelevant. The only cards that count are those in his five-card hand.

Summary

Blind bets placed

Initial deal – two cards face down to each player

First betting round

The flop – three community cards are dealt

Second betting round

The turn – a fourth community card is dealt

Third betting round

The river – the fifth community card is dealt

Final betting round

Showdown

Example

There are five players A, B, C, D, E

A is the dealer
B makes the small blind (£1)
C makes the big blind (£2)

The first two cards are dealt face down. The players look at their cards. C bets £2, D calls, E folds, A raises £2, B calls, C calls, D calls.

The first three community cards are dealt. They are Q, 5, 8

The second betting round commences.

D bets, A raises, B fold, C calls.

The fourth community card is dealt, the board is now Qh, 5c, 8h, 9h.

The third betting round commences.

D bets, A raises, C raises, D folds, A calls.

The fifth community card is dealt, the board is now Qh, 5c, 8h, 9h, 2d.

A bets, C raises, A calls, C raises, A folds.

C is the winner.

Omaha

Each player receives four cards face down. Five cards are then placed face up in the centre of the table to be used by all the players. Each player uses any two cards in his hand and three of the community cards to make the best five-card poker hand. Only two of the player's hole cards can be part of the five-card poker hand. The game is dealt in a similar way to Texas hold 'em with a flop of three cards and blind bets. What makes the game more complicated is the way in which the five-card poker hand is made. When you see the cards you need to give some thought as to what hand you have actually got. At first glance, you may seem to have an exceptionally good hand. But you need to remember that you may only use two of your hole cards (see Figure 9.1).

community cards

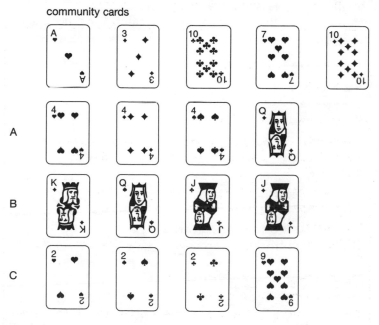

figure 9.1 example hands in Omaha

By looking at the cards in total, player A can immediately see a full house (three fours and two tens). However, because only two cards can be used from his hand, he only has two pair (two tens and two fours).

Player B appears to have a straight (A, K, Q, J, 10) but the hand actually held is two pair (two jacks and two tens).

At first glance, player C may appear to have a full house (three twos and two tens). However, he can only use two cards from his hand so only holds two pair (two tens and two twos).

Caribbean stud poker

The games we have looked at so far all involve betting against the other players – you have to beat everyone else playing in order to win the pot. Caribbean stud poker differs because it is a banking game. Instead of playing against other players, you are playing against the casino, which acts as a banker, paying out all winning bets. The casino provides a dealer. In order to win, you have only to beat the dealer's hand. The other players' hands do not affect the outcome of your bets.

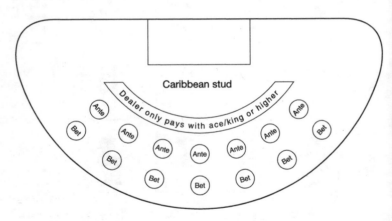

figure 9.2 Caribbean stud layout

The game

The object of the game is to win by having a five-card poker hand that ranks higher than the dealer's. Each player makes an ante-bet and is dealt five cards face down. The dealer receives four cards face down and one card face up.

Players then look at their cards and have the option to play or fold. If a player folds, his ante-bet is lost. If a player decides to continue, he must then make a further bet of double his ante-bet.

The dealer will then reveal his hand. He must have an ace and a king or higher in order to play his hand. If a player's hand beats the dealer's, the ante-bet is paid at evens. See Table 9.1 for the odds for the second bet. If the dealer does not have at least an ace and a king then the player is paid even money on the ante-bet and the additional bet is void (not lost). If, however, the dealer's hand beats the player's, then both bets are lost.

One pair or less	1/1 (even)
Two pair	2/1
Three of a kind	3/1
Straight	4/1
Flush	5/1
Full house	7/1
Four of a kind	20/1
Straight flush	50/1
Royal flush	100/1

table 9.1 payout odds for an additional bet in Caribbean stud poker

If the dealer and the player play the same poker hand, the remaining cards are taken into consideration. If all five cards are equal, the hand is void (the bet is not lost). Neither the ante-bet nor the additional bet is paid. The type of suit makes no difference to the hand.

The disadvantage of this game is that you are relying purely on luck. There is no skill involved. You do not have the opportunity to bluff. In poker games where you are playing for a pot, you are still able to win even with a poor hand but with Caribbean stud poker, if you have a poor hand, you stand little chance of winning.

The minimum odds in this game are evens. In a normal game of poker with, for example, seven players you would have odds of at least 6/1 and quite often a great deal better. The odds paid for the additional bet are also poor compared to the chances of achieving them. Odds of 100/1 are paid for a royal flush, yet your chances of being dealt one are 649,739/1. The only advantage you have is that you know how much each game is going to cost you.

Caribbean stud poker should be played only for amusement purposes. If you want to win money, you are better advised to play games where you are contesting for a pot.

Pai gow poker

In pai gow poker each player in turn has the option of being banker. The game is a mixture of the Chinese game pai gow and American poker. It is played with one deck of 52 cards, plus one joker. The joker can be used only as an ace or to complete a straight, a flush, a straight flush or a royal flush.

The casino provides the dealer. Each player is dealt seven cards. The cards are arranged to make two hands: a two-card hand and a five-card hand. The five-card hand must rank higher or be equal to the two-card hand (see Table 9.2).

The object of the game is for both your hands to rank higher than both those of your opponent. Your two-card hand must rank higher than your opponent's two-card hand and your five card hand must rank higher than that of your opponent.

Five-card hand	Two-card hand
Five aces (five aces plus the joker)	One pair
Royal flush	High card
Straight flush	
Four of a kind	
Full house	
Flush	
Straight	
Three of a kind	
Two pair	
One pair	
High card	

table 9.2 ranking of hands in pai gow poker

If one of your hands ranks the same as your opponent's hand, this is a tie (or copy hand). The banker wins all ties. If you win one hand but lose the other, this is known as a 'push'. In a push, no money is exchanged. Winning hands are paid even money less a 5 per cent commission. Losing hands lose the money bet.

The game

The dealer and each player in turn are all given the opportunity to be banker. You can only be banker if you bet against the dealer the last time he was banker. You need to have sufficient chips to pay the bets should your opponent win.

You arrange your cards into the two hands and place them face down on the table. Once you've put them down, you may no longer touch them. The dealer will turn over his cards and make his hands. Each hand is compared to the dealer's hands. If the player wins one hand and loses the other, the bet is void. If you wrongly set your hand – you lose. The major disadvantage to this game is that you are relying on the luck of the deal – there is no skill involved, If your cards are poor, there is no opportunity to bluff. The dealer plays his hand if he has the minimum required and does not drop out of the betting.

As with Caribbean stud poker, the odds are also poor compared to playing for a pot.

See Figure 9.3. Player A has beaten the dealer's five-card hand but has failed to beat the two-card hand. This is a push – the money bet is not lost.

dealer's hands

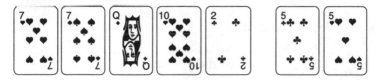

player's hands

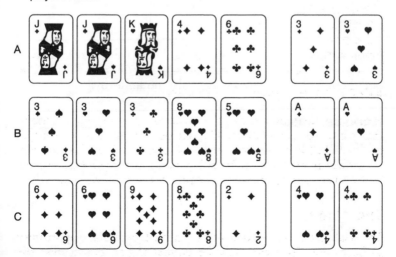

figure 9.3 example hands in pai gow poker

Player B has beaten both hands. His bet is paid at even money less 5 per cent commission.

Player C has failed to beat the dealer's five and two-card hand. He loses his bet.

Three-card poker/progressive poker

Three-card poker is a banking game played in casinos. The house advantage is less than 3.5 per cent. There is no strategy involved with three-card poker, the player simply decides how much to bet. Three-card poker consists of two games that are played either separately or together – three-card ante/play and pair plus. It is played with a standard pack of 52 cards. With the pair plus game the aim is to make a ranking poker hand that is paid out at fixed odds.

With the ante-bet the aim is to make a three-card poker hand that beats the dealer's hand. The dealer needs to have at least a queen high to qualify.

The dealer and player are both dealt three cards. Pair plus bets are paid out according to the payout odds.

Ante and play

Players can also place an ante-bet against the dealer. After the cards are dealt, they can place a play bet equal to the initial ante-bet.

As only three cards are used, the rankings are not the same as traditional poker. A straight ranks higher than a flush. Aces rank both high and low. There is also no mini-royal flush.

Hand rankings

Straight flush
Three of a kind
Straight
Flush
Pair
High card

Payout odds

Pair plus
Pair 1/1
Flush 4/1
Straight 6/1
Three of a kind 30/1
Straight flush 40/1

Ante-bonus

Straight 1/1
Three of a kind 4/1
Straight flush 5/1

Four-card poker

This game is similar to three-card poker. The player makes an initial bet called the 'ante-wager'. Players are dealt five cards and have to make their best four-card poker hand. The dealer is dealt six cards – five face down and one face up. He uses the six cards to make his best four-card poker hand. There are also variants where the player gets six cards and the dealer gets seven.

After looking at his cards, the player can then make an additional bet up to three times the initial bet this is called the 'play wager'. Alternatively, he can fold and will lose his ante wager. The players hand must equal or beat the dealer's to win. If the player wins, both bets are paid at odds of even money. For high-ranking hands, the ante-wager is paid at the odds shown. There is also an additional bet called 'aces up wager' that the player can make if his hand is a pair of aces or higher. The ranking of the hands is different from that of traditional poker.

Ranking of hands

Royal flush
Four of a kind
Straight flush
Three of a kind
Straight
Two pair
Flush
One pair

High card

Ante-wager	Bonus	Aces up
Four of a kind	25/1	
Straight flush	20/1	
Three of a kind	2/1	9/1
Flush		6/1
Straight		4/1
Two pair		2/1
Pair of aces		1/1

table 9.3 odds for four-card poker

Let it ride

Let it ride poker is a banking game. The aim is to get a pair of tens or better using three cards dealt to the player and two community cards dealt to the dealer.

The player makes three equal bets. The dealer then gives each player three cards and the dealer is dealt two community cards face down. After seeing their first three cards, the player may take back one of their three bets or let it ride. The dealer then turns over one of the community cards. The player then has the option to take out another bet or let it ride. The dealer then turns over the second community card. If the player fails to get at least a pair of tens, all bets are lost. If a hand containing at least a pair of tens is held, bets are then paid out according to Table 9.4.

Tens or over	1/1
Two pair	2/1
Three of a kind	3/1
Straight	5/1
Flush	8/1
Full house	11/1
Four of a kind	50/1
Straight flush	200/1
Royal flush	1000/1
House advantage	3.5%

table 9.4 let it ride odds

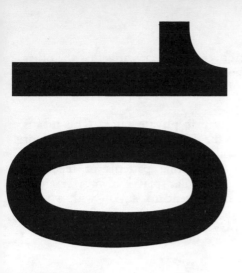

10

playing strategies

In this chapter you will learn:
- five-card strategies
- five-card stud strategies
- seven-card stud strategies
- Texas hold 'em strategies
- Omaha strategies
- Caribbean stud poker strategies
- pai gow poker strategies.

Five-card draw

In five-card draw you do not see any of the cards that the other player can use to make their hands. The only indications that you have are the number of cards they exchange and how they tackle the betting.

Five-card draw is mostly played in private games. This means that you are likely to know the other players fairly well. Your knowledge of the players will help you to decide the action to take. Look out for repetitive betting patterns or repetitive methods of play. Does a particular player always retain a kicker? Does a particular player tend to stay in with a poor hand, hoping to improve on the draw? Does a player always fold poor hands and only play with good initial hands?

What hand should you play?

Five-card draw can generally be won with a high pair. If you get a high pair in the initial deal, it may be enough to win the pot without any improvement. If you get a low pair in the initial deal, chances are someone else already has a high pair. If, for example, you stay in with a pair of sixes and take three cards in an attempt to get three of a kind, the odds against your achieving your desired hand are 7.5/1. Your opponent may already have a pair of jacks and also has the same chance as you of improving. However, if neither of you improves, he has already beaten your hand.

A good initial hand has a greater chance of winning than a poor initial hand. If you compare the odds of being dealt a good hand in the first deal to the odds of improving on cards already held (see Table 10.1), you can see that you have a much better chance of being initially dealt a good hand than improving.

So, if, in the first deal, you have nothing, it is better to withdraw from the game instead of exchanging all five cards. Even exchanging four cards needs nothing short of a miracle to give you a good hand. You will be betting against players who may already hold good cards and who, by exchanging one or two, can also improve.

The hand that most people will tend to aim for is three of a kind. If you have a high pair, the only real threat will come from someone with three of a kind. The higher ranking hands of a straight and above are rare.

Hand held	Cards drawn	Desired hand	Odds against achieving hand
Three of a kind	2	any improvement	17/2
Three of a kind + kicker	1	any improvement	11/1
Three of a kind	1	full house	15/1
Three of a kind	1	four of a kind	46/1
Three of a kind	2	full house	15/1
Three of a kind	2	four of a kind	23/1
Two pair	1	full house	11/1
One pair	3	three of a kind	7.5/1
One pair	3	full house	97/1
One pair	3	four of a kind	359/1
One pair + kicker	2	any improvement	3/1
One pair + kicker	2	two pair using kicker	7.5/1
One pair + kicker	2	two pair without kicker	17/1
One pair + kicker	2	three of a kind	12/1
One pair + kicker	2	full house	119/1
One pair + kicker	2	fours	1080/1
Four-card flush	1	pair	3/1
Four-card flush	1	flush	4.5/1
Four-card incomplete straight flush (open ended)	1	straight or flush	2/1
		straight flush	22.5/1
Incomplete straight	1	any improvement	1/1
Flush (inside)		pair	3/1
		flush	5/1
		straight	11/1
		straight flush	46/1

table 10.1 odds against improving hands in draw poker

What have the other players got?

The number of cards that the other players decide to discard will give you an indication of the sort of hand that they have. You will need to bear in mind that they may not be trying to achieve the most obvious hand and may bluff.

Someone who discards no cards is indicating that their hand is fine as it is. They could have anything from a straight or higher or they could be bluffing. Because the higher hands appear extremely rarely, someone who uses this tactic too often is most likely bluffing. A tight player (someone who tends to wait for a good hand before playing) would need to be regarded with more respect if they do not discard cards. They may just have a huge hand.

A player who discards one card shows that he needs just one card to complete his hand. He could be aiming to make anything from a straight or higher or could be bluffing. If he needs one card to complete a straight and fails his hand may be worthless and may just end up as a high card. He may also match one of his cards for a pair. He could have two pair and need one card to make a full house. If he fails he will have just two pair. Your knowledge of the player may give you some indication of whether or not he has made his desired hand. A tight player will be most likely to fold if the hand is not made. Others will try to bluff that they did get what they wanted.

A rarer possibility is that he has four of a kind and will discard one card to make you think he is going for a straight.

A player who discards two cards shows that they have a possibility of a three of a kind but are just as likely to have a pair. It is a common tactic when you have just a pair to try to disguise this fact by discarding two cards and keeping a kicker. A kicker is the highest other card. Suppose you are dealt K, K, A, 3, 8. To disguise the fact that you have a pair, you discard the 3 and the 8 and keep the ace. The ace is a high card and you may get a match in the draw for a possible two pair or a full house. By retaining a kicker you make it less likely that you will achieve a four of a kind but you keep the other players guessing about what your hand is.

Discarding two cards may also indicate that the player has three cards to a straight. Their chances of making the straight will be better if it is open ended.

A player who discards three cards shows that they have nothing better than a pair. A player who already has a high pair or three of a kind knows at this stage that he has probably beaten this player.

How many cards should you exchange?

Depending on your hand, you will need to decide the best strategy for discarding cards. Your position in the betting will need to be considered. If it is your turn to act first, you have no knowledge of what the other players' hands may be. You will have to judge how good your hand is based on probabilities. How likely is your hand to get beaten? If you are in a late position and all the other players have acted, you have the opportunity to modify your action based on what has already happened. If all the other players have discarded three cards, you will know that no one has currently got anything better than a pair. If you have a high pair or three of a kind or higher then you know you have the strongest hand.

If players are discarding two cards, to show strength you need to also discard two or less. If you discard three cards, you show weakness.

From the last position, even if your hand is poor, you have an ideal opportunity to pull off a bluff. If the other players are showing weakness, they are more likely to fold. Discarding no cards or just one gives the message that either you have a huge hand or you have the possibility of making a huge hand.

Holding a pair

If you are holding a pair, you can improve your hand by exchanging up to three cards. However, if you exchange three cards, the other players will be immediately aware that you are likely to have a pair. Anyone with two pair or three of a kind will be confident that he has a better hand.

Instead of drawing three cards, you have the option of keeping a kicker (see earlier). Instead of exchanging three cards, you exchange two. Your chances of improving your hand are slightly reduced, but now the other players will be unsure as to whether you only have a pair or a possible three of a kind.

However, do not fall into the pattern of always retaining a kicker when you have a pair as the other players will soon work out your strategy. Vary your play as much as possible so that your opponents are never sure about your hand.

You may decide that the time is right to pull off a bluff. You may decide to take just one card to give an indication of a possible two pair that you are trying to improve to a full house or a possible flush. A big raise after drawing cards would be needed to back up the bluff.

Alternatively, you may decide to take no cards. The players will be aware that you may have been dealt a very good hand, but again, they cannot be certain. They will be aware of the odds against your obtaining a high-ranking hand with just five cards, but if you are known as a player who rarely bluffs then you may be successful. However, if you have bluffed too often in the past, you are unlikely to get away with another bluff.

Holding three of a kind

You have the choice of exchanging either one or both cards. You have a greater chance of improving to a full house or four of a kind by taking two cards.

Holding a full house

It is pointless trying to improve to four of a kind. You already hold a hand that is going to be very difficult for other players to beat and so your real decision should be whether to raise before the draw to force out other players who may improve on the draw.

Getting a poor draw

If, after the draw, you still have a poor hand, you can either fold or bluff. If there are still lots of players left in the game, it will be better to fold. It is easier to convince one or two players that you got your hand than lots.

Five-card stud

In five-card stud, you progressively get more information on which to base your decisions. Once all the cards have been dealt, you should have a pretty good idea of your opponents' likely hands.

Strategy

Each player need to assess their chances of winning against the other hands. A high pair is generally enough to win a game.

Most players will be aiming to improve a pair to three of a kind. Higher hands, ranking a straight or above, are rare. Bearing this in mind, if you cannot match or better the highest card showing, you should fold.

In the initial deal, you see one of the player's cards. If, at this stage, they have a pair, you can immediately see what that pair may be. They may show an ace, indicating that they have the possibility of having a pair of aces. You may also see a card that matches yours. For example, if your hole card is an ace and another player has an ace showing, you know immediately that your chances of getting another ace are diminished.

As more cards are dealt, the possible hands held and the potential hands become more obvious. After the third card is dealt, you can see if anyone has a potential for a three of a kind. If the two face-up cards are matched, then there is a possible three of a kind. If one of their matching cards is in another player's hand then they have less of a chance of making the hand. At each stage, you need to compare your hand with those of the other players and decide if it is worthwhile continuing or better to fold.

See Figure 10.1. In the initial deal, player B has the lowest face-up card so makes a forced bet. At this stage, player D is showing the strongest hand and could have a pair of aces. Player A is showing a lower card but could have a pair of jacks. B could have a pair of fives and C could have a pair of sevens. If D has a pair of aces he knows he has the best hand. However, if he only has one ace, he knows that if any of the other players has a pair, they are already beating him.

As each card is dealt, more information is known about each player's hand. By the third card, player A can have nothing more than a pair of jacks, player B can have nothing more than a pair of fives. Player C potentially has a pair of aces and player D has potentially a pair of aces. Because there are two aces showing on the board in two different players' hands, there is a reduced chance that either of these players will make a three of a kind with their aces.

By the fourth card players A, C and D are all showing pairs. Player B has the potential to achieve a straight flush. Player A is showing the highest pair with eights and the potential for two pair with jacks and eights or three of a kind with eights. Both C and D are showing the potential for either two pair or three of a kind. If player A has three eights, then he knows at this stage that he has the highest hand. If player C has another seven, then he knows that only player A has the possibility of having a higher hand at this stage. He can see that player B has a seven, which means he has no chance to make four of a kind. In order to win from this point, he would need to force out the other players to stop them from improving. If player D's hole card is a six, he will have three of a kind at this stage. He knows at this stage that if A and C only have a pair or two pair, he has beaten them. In order to win from this point, he would need to force out all the other players before they get the chance to improve.

By the time the fifth card has been dealt, it is clear what the possible hands might be. The best hands are A – three of a kind with eights, B – a straight flush, C – three of a kind with sevens and D – four of a kind with sixes. If each player achieves his best possible hand, then player B would win on a showdown.

If player B does not make his flush and folds, then players A, C and D are left. If player D does not have four of a kind, then his strategy will be based on whether or not he believes that A or C have a three of a kind. If A or C have two pair, they can see that they are beaten by player D, who is showing three of a kind. Suppose A folds. Then C and D are left. If C has three of a kind with sevens, he knows that he has beaten D's three of a kind with sixes but will not beat four of a kind with sixes or a full house (three sixes and two aces). However, C knows that the chances of D actually having four of a kind or a full house are remote. An ace is shown in player C's hand, which reduces the chance of D having a full house.

If player A has another 8, he is certain of beating player C. He also knows that if B has any card other than a diamond, then his hand is nothing. If player D's hole card (the card dealt face down) is not a 6 or an ace, then player A will also beat him. One of the aces is revealed in player C's hand, which gives D less chance of achieving a full house.

Player B knows that he has potentially the best hand. If his hole card is not a diamond then whether or not he wins will depend on how well he can bluff.

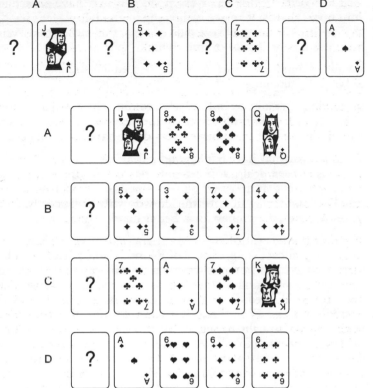

figure 10.1 example hands in five-card stud

Seven-card stud

Like five-card stud, you gradually get more information about each player's hand as the game progresses. In low-limit games it can be harder to force players to fold and they will often stay in to a showdown. In these games, you should therefore play hands that have a good chance of winning in a showdown.

At the start of the game you should aim to only play with a good initial hand. Ideally, your lowest card should equal or be higher than any other card showing. You should play hands that have a good chance of improving to better hands so three of a kind, three cards to a flush, three cards to a straight or a high pair indicate a good start.

If one of the cards you need is showing in another player's hand then it is better to fold. For example, you may have an ace in your pocket cards. If an ace is showing in another player's hand, chances are they may have a pair of aces, this means that your hand has a poor chance of improving.

If you are aiming for a straight, an open-ended straight is going to be easier to complete than a closed straight.

If you don't get a good initial hand, folding early will save you money. It is useless progressing all the way to a showdown on the off-chance that the other players don't have better hands.

Although you may have had a good initial hand, if, after further cards have been dealt, you get nothing to improve your hand and it appears that the other players' hands have improved, you should fold. Staying in until the showdown will be costly. It is better to save your money for a better hand.

Three of a kind will often be good enough to win a hand. If, early on, you have a high three of a kind, chances are it will be high enough to win on a showdown. In this case, you want to keep everyone betting for as long as possible to maximize the pot. You will need to look out for players who have the possibility of a higher three of a kind or look like they may improve to a straight or higher. In this case, you will need to raise to get them to fold. If you have a low three of a kind early on, you will need to try to force out anyone who has the possibility of improving to a higher three of a kind.

Suppose you have three sevens and another player is showing a pair of jacks, you need to force this player out before they improve to three jacks.

Occasionally, you will be in a situation when you know that a player can't possibly have their desired hands. For example, two players may each show an ace, but you have the other two aces in your pocket cards. If one of these players folds, the other may try to pull off a bluff and raise early, hoping to convince you that he has three aces. This may be enough to force out the other players, but you know that the best that he can possibly have is a lower pair. Although you have no chance of improving your aces, if the other player gets no decent cards you know that you have most likely beaten him.

Figure 10.2 example hands in seven-card stud

See Figure 10.2. Suppose you are player A. You have two pair. You can immediately see that player B has a better hand with three of a kind; player C also has two pair, which beats your hand, but could have a full house if he has either another king or another 5. In the cards that you are showing, you have the 9, 8 and 7 of hearts. The 10 of hearts and the 5 of hearts are showing in B's and C's hands. This makes it impossible to achieve the straight flush. A straight is a possibility but as three of the tens are shown in B's hand and two of the fives are shown in C's hand, so this cuts down the chances of making a straight. A would be better off folding this hand. B is showing three of a kind with tens. His best possible hand would be four of a kind followed by a full house. C is showing two pair with kinds over fives. His best possible hand would be four of a kind with kings, followed by four of a kind with fives, followed by a full house. C is likely to stay in until the river in the hope of getting either another king or another 5. With no improvement, B will win in a showdown.

Texas hold 'em

Since you do not get to see the player's pocket cards, the only indication you have of their possible hands is the way in which they are betting.

The number and experience of the players will have an influence on the strategy that you need to use. With a large number of players, you need to bear in mind that the competition for a good hand will be greater and there is a greater likelihood that one of the players is going to have a good hand. Where there are lots of players and you have a decent hand, you need to try and cut down the competition as early as possible to ensure that those with mediocre hands fold before they get the opportunity to improve. If you are playing with less experienced players, they are more likely to stay in the game for longer and not fold. In such games, you need to be certain that you are playing a good hand that has a very good chance in a showdown as you are much more likely to end up in one. In order to make a proper assessment, you really need to see all the community cards first. However, if you always stay in the game until all the community cards have been dealt, in the long run you will lose money. The trick with hold 'em is to learn to fold early when your hand shows little promise and only continue to the showdown with good hands.

Strategy before the flop

You need to decide whether or not your two cards are worth playing. In general terms, it is worthwhile playing any pair, consecutive cards of the same suit, such as 9, 8 or 6, 5 and fairly high cards of the same suit such as J, 9.

A pair gives you the opportunity to improve to three or four of a kind and opens the possibility to a full house. Consecutive cards of the same suit lead to the possibility of a flush or a straight. High cards of the same suit open the possibility for a flush or a straight.

Strategy after the flop

You now have a better indication of the possible hands. You can assess your position against all the other possibilities, If the community cards have not helped you, they may well have given other players the possibility of a really good hand. If this is the situation, then fold now. Suppose you have a pair of fives and the flop gives Ah, Qh, Jh. Chances are that someone has stayed in with an ace or a queen or a jack. Anyone who now has a pair of aces, a pair of queens or a pair of jacks has already beaten your hand. Someone may also now have three aces, three queens or three jacks. Since all the community cards are hearts this opens the possibility of a flush or a straight.

Suppose you have a pair of fives and a flop of 8s, 5c, 2h, you now have three fives. The only danger would come from someone with a three eights. The cards are of different suits so it doesn't help anyone looking for a flush or a straight flush. You are still in a fairly good position. You now need to eliminate as much competition as possible. Another player may hold a high pair like a pair of kings or queens. You need to raise to get them out of the game. If they stay in, they could improve to three kings or three queens, which would beat you on a showdown.

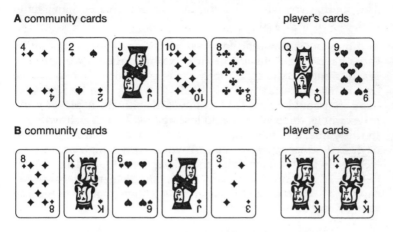

A community cards   player's cards

B community cards   player's cards

figure 10.3 'nuts'

Nuts

Occasionally a situation may arise where you know that you have the best possible hand (nuts) that can be made using the community cards. There is no way that you can be beaten. Clearly, in this situation you want to maximize the pot. Your strategy for betting will need to be based on your knowledge of the players. You need to keep the betting at the right level to keep as many of the players betting for as long as possible.

Suppose you have Ah, Jh, and the flop is Kh, Qh, 10h, you know at this stage that you have the best possible hand and that no one else can beat you. Chances are someone else will have at least a pair of kings or a pair of queens. You don't need to force anyone out. If doesn't matter how many people stay in until the showdown as you will win it. You have two choices. You can slow play your hand and call until the last betting round.

You then raise when you reach the final betting round. Anyone who has paid to get this far will likely want to stay in to the showdown.

Alternatively, you can start raising on the flop. Anyone with a king or a queen will likely stay in with the hope of improving. Anyone with an ace will stay in, hoping to get a straight. They know that there is a possibility of a royal flush but will understand that the chances of anyone making it are rare. If you raise now, chances are they will still stay in to the showdown. The pot that you win will therefore be much greater than a hand that was slow played.

You may not know that you have nuts until all the community cards have been dealt. In the first example, the player does not get nuts until all the community cards are dealt. Then he can see that he has the straight Q, J, 10, 9, 8. This is the best possible hand that could be made with the cards shown. A player with, for example, three jacks would lose against him in a showdown. In this game, a number of players may have stayed in. The flop of 4, 2, J was nothing special. Anyone with a high pair would likely stay in. The jack helps the player with Q, 9. The straight needs a 10 and any king or any 8 will complete it. After the next card, the 10 is there. The player now knows that he needs any king or any 8.

In the second example, the player has three kings, the best possible hand. The third king comes in the flop. You have two choices: you can slow play (not raise) the hand or start raising. If you slow play, you take the risk that anyone with pocket eights or pocket sixes will likely go all the way to the showdown and may get a fourth card on the way. A player with pocket aces is likely to stay in to the river hoping to get another ace. It is therefore a better strategy to start raising. A raise may help to cut the competition. Even if it fails to cut the competition, it will maximize the pot.

See Figure 10.4. The best possible hand from the community cards showing is four of a kind with aces, followed by a full house then three of a kind.

Player A will deduce that he has a good hand with three of a kind. He knows that he has the best possible three of a kind and can only be beaten by a full house and since he holds one of the aces, the chances of anyone holding another ace are low. To complete a full house, someone would need either two queens, two fours or two threes or to have the other ace with a queen, four or three.

community cards

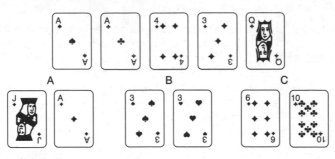

figure 10.4 example hands in hold 'em

However, player B has a full house. He knows that only four of a kind or a full house with queens or fours could beat him.

Player C has nothing and would be wise to fold.

If players A and B both reach the showdown, B would win.

Omaha

The strategy is similar to that of Texas hold 'em. You really need to see the flop before you can make any decision. However a, situation can arise when it is wise to fold immediately after you have been dealt your hole cards.

Being dealt four of a kind in your hole cards is one of the worst possible situations. You can only use two cards so at best you have a pair with no chance of improving on them. Being dealt three of a kind also gives you only a remote chance that the fourth card will appear in the community cards. The same is true of being dealt four cards to a possible flush; your chances of making the flush are drastically reduced.

The best cards to play with are high pairs or high cards of the same suit (if you hold only two of the same suit), which could lead to a flush.

After the flop, you will be in a much better position to judge your chances of winning. Then you can assess all the possibilities and work out your chances of making a good hand.

figure 10.5 hands to fold on in Omaha

It is at this stage that you need to force out anyone who has the potential to improve his or her hand into one that could beat yours.

Nuts

As with Texas hold 'em, occasionally a situation may arise where you know that you have the best possible hand (nuts) that can be made using the community cards. There is no way that you can be beaten. Clearly, in this situation you want to maximize the pot. Your strategy for betting will need to be based on your knowledge of the players. You need to keep betting at the right level to keep as many players betting as possible.

Caribbean stud poker

Caribbean stud poker has a house advantage of 5.26 per cent. By playing the following strategy it is possible to cut the house advantage to about 2.6 per cent. You need to decide whether to play or fold your hand. You should fold if you don't get a minimum hand of an ace and a king. Players should raise when they hold any pair or an ace and a king. With some hands you need to match the dealer's up card to reduce the possibility that the dealer has a pair.

Player's hand	Dealer's hand	Action
Lower than A K		Fold
Any pair	Any up card	Raise
A K Q J x	Any up card	Raise
A K Q xx	Must match one card	Raise
A K J xx	Must match one card	Raise
A K 10 xx	Must match one card	Raise

table 10.2 details for the hands that should be raised

The £1 progressive jackpot bet it extremely difficult to win. It is not worthwhile playing until the level of the jackpot exceeds £263,000.

Pai gow poker

The strategy for pai gow poker is based on how you set the hands. The five-card hand needs to be higher than the two-card hand. There will be situations where, for example, you have two pair. Depending on the cards, it is sometimes advantageous to split up the two pair and put the high pair in the back hand and the low pair in the front hand. The following gives the strategy for setting the hands with the various different combinations of cards.

Five-card hand = back
Two-card hand = front

No pair:
Back – highest card
Front – second and third highest cards

One pair:
Back – pair
Front – highest other two cards

Two pair:
• A A, K K, Q Q, J J:
Back – high pair
Front – small pair

- 7, 7 to 10, 10 with an ace:

Back – two pair

Front – Ace

- 2, 2 to 6, 6 with a king:

Back – two pair

Front – king

- 2, 2 to 6, 6 with no king:

Back – high pair

Front – low pair.

Three pair:

Back – low pairs

Front – high pair

Three of a kind:

- With aces:

Back – pair of aces

Front – ace and next highest card

Two sets of three of a kind:

Back – the lower three of a kind

Front – pair from the higher set

Straight, flush, straight flush:

- With no pair:

Back – complete hand

Front – Two highest other cards

- With one pair:

Back – complete hand

Front – Two highest other cards

- With two pair:

Use two-pair strategy

- With three of a kind:

Back – complete hand

Front – pair

Full house:

Front – pair

Four of a kind:

- Jacks to aces – split; 7 to 10 with an ace:

Back – four of a kind

Front – ace

- 7 to 10 no ace – split; 6 or below – do not split

- With three of a kind:
Back – full house
Front – highest pair

Five aces:
Back – three aces
Front – pair of aces

Example

With the following cards: K, J, 3, K, 9, 7, J there is a possible hand of two pair. This would be set as follows:

Back – K, K, 9, 7, 3
Front – J, J

Let it ride strategy

The decisions you need to make with let it ride are whether or not to leave the first and second bets in play.

You should let the first bet ride if your first three cards are:

a pair of tens or better
any three cards to a royal flush
three-card straight flush or inside straight flush
three-card double inside straight flush with two high cards (10 or higher)
10, J, Q.

You should let the second bet ride if your first four cards are:

pair of tens or better
any four cards of the same suit
four-card straight (open end)
four high cards (10 or higher).

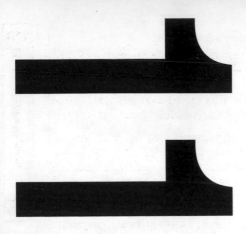

11

playing in private games

In this chapter you will learn:
- about advantages and disadvantages of private games
- how to host a game
- table etiquette
- strategies for play.

Private games

Poker is widely played in private games outside casinos and card rooms. These games often take place in someone's home. Groups of friends will regularly meet on a Friday night to play poker around the kitchen table. It is an enjoyable social game that can be played just for fun or as a gambling game for money.

Private games are an excellent training ground for learning poker. Initially, you can play just for fun without the risk of losing money. You can try out lots of different games until you find one that suits you. You can experiment with different strategies and find what works best for you. As you gain more confidence and skill, you can try out small stake games. With greater experience you can graduate to higher stake games or try-out tournaments.

There are advantages and disadvantages to playing poker in a private game. Playing in a private game is cheaper than going to a casino. There is no rake, hourly rate or admission fee to pay. You don't have to worry about a dress code. However, with private games there is a limit to the amount you can win. You are limited to the bankroll of your fellow players. In a casino, there are many players with large bankrolls. In casinos, there are games going on sometimes 24 hours a day. With private games, you may be limited to one a week.

Private games run the risk that they may get raided by the police and stopped. Your actions may be entirely legitimate but the host may have done something to break the law by, for example, advertising the game. A game may be even curtailed by the host's irate spouse who does not agree with gambling taking place in their home.

The playing of poker in private games has resulted in many different forms of the game. This is because each group of players modifies the game by incorporating its own rules. This changing of the rules means that private games are more prone to end in disputes. Arguments can easily ensue about the finer points of the rules. With large amounts of money at stake, disputes can easily escalate into violent conflicts.

Private games are also more vulnerable to cheating. There are numerous methods for cheating at poker. Before playing in a private game, you should be aware of all the different ways that it is possible to cheat, as described in Chapter 8. You should take all the necessary precautions to ensure that you are not a victim of cheating. You need to take particular care if you are playing with strangers. If their luck seems too good to be true then chances are there is some cheating going on. If you doubt the integrity of any of the other players it is best to quit playing. Cash in your chips and go home. Accusations of cheating can lead to bad feeling and even violence.

In games in a casino or card room, it is much easier to quit playing. In private games, if you have won a lot of money, the other players are more likely to try to persuade you into continuing to play. They may complain that you need to be fair and give them a chance to win back their money.

The law

Depending on where you live, playing poker in private games may or may not be legal. Private games are often categorized as social gaming. Before playing in a private game, you should check whether or not it is legal where you live. In areas where poker is banned, there are often underground clubs operating. However, if poker is played illegally, there is a danger that the premises could get raided by the police and the game closed down. Most jurisdictions tend to prosecute the operators of illegal games rather than the players. However, if a place is raided players are likely to lose their bankroll. Where poker in private games is legal, there are frequently restrictions on the charging of a rake or hourly rate. Often this is not allowed. It is also common for there to be a ban on the advertising, of private games. While it may be acceptable to invite your friends to your home to play, it is often not allowed to find players through advertising, for example, in the local newspaper or with flyers.

UK law

The UK has liberal gaming laws. In the UK, poker may be played in a private dwelling but not in a public place. You can, therefore, invite your friends to play in your home but not, for example, in a place where the public is admitted, such as your local community centre. If you do play in your home, you are not allowed to make any commercial gain or, in other words, run a poker game as a business. This means that you cannot profit from the game by charging the players an hourly rate, rake or admission fee. Anyone who makes commercial gain from poker must have the appropriate permission from the gaming board and operate on licensed premises.

Poker can also be played in a private members' club. The club must have at least 25 members and must be formed for the general benefit of its members. It cannot be formed for commercial gain. If the club is registered by the licensing authority then members can be charged up to £2 per day. Unregistered clubs can only charge 60p per day. Gaming cannot be the main principle for which the club is established or conducted. No bankers' games are allowed. This means you could play games like five-card draw, five-card stud, seven-card stud, Texas hold 'em and Omaha but games like Caribbean stud and pai gow poker would not be allowed.

Poker can also be played for charity or good causes. No banking games can be played. All the money raised, less reasonable costs for providing facilities for the games, must be applied to purposes other than private gain. Players are allowed to make one payment of £4, there is no limit on stakes, but these must all be returned to the winners. Prizes or awards in cash and kind may be made by the promoters up to a maximum value of £400.

US law

In the United States, each state has its own gambling laws. Some states allow social gambling and others ban it. Social gambling is generally considered gambling that takes place between individuals where only the individuals can benefit by winning. Where social gambling is allowed, it is not permitted to make a commercial gain so you cannot charge an hourly rate, rake or admission fee.

The states that currently allow social gambling include: Alabama, Alaska, Arizona, California, Colorado, Connecticut, Delaware, Florida ($10 limit), Hawaii, Kentucky, Louisiana, Maine, Minnesota, Montana, Nevada, New Jersey, New Mexico, New York, North Dakota, Ohio, Oregon, South Carolina, Texas, Virginia, Washington and Wyoming. In other states, social gambling is either banned or the situation is unclear. With the advent of internet gambling, many states are currently reviewing their gambling laws, so, before playing, you should check the current legal situation.

Deciding the rules

Poker can be played in myriad ways. The rules in private games are unwritten. They are likely built up over time between a group of players. If you start playing with such a group, one that is used to playing together, it is likely that they have introduced their own variations into the game. Before you start playing, have a full discussion about the rules. Do not start playing until you fully understand them. It is much easier to lay down the rules before playing than trying to sort them out when there is a dispute. You should also initially watch a few games so that you can familiarize yourself with their way of doing things.

Just because the players call a game by a particular name, for example Texas hold 'em, don't assume that they will play the game with the same rules that you find in casinos. Just about every aspect of the game can be changed. There may be different ways of ranking the hands. Hands other than the standard rankings may be used. Any number of wildcards may be used. The jokers, twos or other cards may be wild. The betting structure may also vary. There may or may not be an ante. If there is an ante, it may be set at virtually any amount. The raises may or may not be limited. There may be more or fewer betting rounds. There may be different rules to determine who acts first in a betting round. There may be other rules to determine what happens to folded hands. Players may or may not have the right to look at folded hands. With tied hands there may be rules that take other cards into consideration.

Before you start playing you need to find out exactly what the rules are. The things that you need to know before you settle down to play are:

- What game is being played, e.g. five-card stud, seven-card stud, Texas hold 'em etc.
- Whether the rules for the chosen game are the same or different as the standardized versions and whether they have introduced any additional rules.
- Do they follow the standard ranking of hands?
- Are additional rankings used?
- Are any cards wild? If yes, which cards? If wildcards are used, is five of a kind allowed as a hand?
- Is there an ante? If yes, how much?
- Are blind bets placed? If yes, how much?

- What is the minimum bet?
- What is the maximum bet?
- How much can you raise by?
- Is there a limit to the number of times you can bet in each round?
- Is checking allowed?
- Who bets first in each round?
- What happens if a player runs out of chips?
- What happens at the showdown? Can players with a lower hand than the winner muck their hand without showing it or are all players in the showdown obliged to show their hands?
- What happens if there is a tie? Do the players share the pot? Do other cards count in a showdown? Is there a hierarchy of suits?
- What happens if the cards are misdealt?
- What happens if a card is revealed by the dealer?
- What happens if any cards are revealed or dropped on the floor while playing? Are the hands declared dead?
- Are people allowed to watch the game?

Table etiquette

Private games are much more informal than casino games, but to interfere as little as possible in the game certain manners of behaviour are expected. Although these rules are not written down, players are generally expected to abide by them. They help with the smooth running of the game and reduce the possibilities for cheating.

Cards should be kept in view at all times

Hiding your cards with your hands is generally frowned on. So too is removing your cards from the table. You can't, for example, put them in your pocket. This helps to cut down on cheating. If a player can take their cards out of view, they can easily switch poor-value cards for higher value cards.

Don't act out of turn

Players should only act when it is their turn. If you want to fold your cards, don't just muck them straight away. Wait until it is your turn to bet. If you muck them straight away you give the players before you a greater advantage as they know in advance that you will fold. The players that act after you will get angry as a player that may have folded, may stay in the game with the knowledge that you are folding. If you want to bet, don't put your chips into the pot until it is your turn. If you bet early you also give an advantage to the players acting before you, as they know in advance your intentions. They may fold rather than stay in the game. This means that the pot will be lower. Neither should you tell the other players of any action you intend to take before it is your turn.

Bet clearly

Don't throw chips at the pot. Bet clearly so that everyone can see that you have contributed correctly to the pot. Before placing chips into the pot, you should separate the amount you intend to bet from your chips by placing in the chips to be bet in front of you away from your chips and then add them to the pot. If you need to have change from the pot, show the transaction clearly to avoid any suspicion from the other players.

Don't delay the game

The other players will want to get on and play and will not want to wait for you to finish your sandwiches or to take a break before betting. Causing delays or distractions to the game gives players an ideal opportunity to cheat. Breaks should be taken at mutually agreed times. If you need to leave the table, sit out an entire hand rather than making the other players wait for you.

Identify marked cards

If you see a card that has become marked, for example, if the corner is creased, notify the other players so that a new deck can be used. If you let it slip that you knew another player's hand because of a marked card, you'll be accused of cheating yourself.

Don't reveal cards

If a player reveals any cards in his hand to another player, either deliberately or accidentally, that hand should be declared dead. The hand is automatically folded. Poker relies on the other players not knowing your hand. If you show any of your cards to another player, he then has knowledge that can give him an advantage. If someone is watching a game, do not allow him to view the cards of more than one player. He may give away information about the hand. If the dealer reveals any card while dealing, then that card should be considered dead. It is automatically mucked.

Do not touch another player's cards or chips

Touching another player's cards or chips can lead to accusations of cheating. If a player wins, the winner should collect the pot. This eliminates the possibility of other players stealing chips.

Hosting a private game

If you decide to host a poker game in your home, you will need to ensure that you have the basic necessary equipment and a quiet environment. You don't need specialized equipment to play. A suitable table, chairs and a standard pack of cards with a 52-card deck are all that is needed. A card table covered in felt to stop the cards slipping around is ideal but a table covered with a cloth will also suffice. To cut down on the likelihood of a dealer cheating, you can use a shoe for the dealing of the cards.

Poker can be played with cash but, for ease of play, chips should be used. Sets of poker chips for this purpose can be purchased from specialist game suppliers. At the start of play, each player purchases chips from the host much like in a casino and at the end of play these are exchanged back into cash. Using chips helps the game run more smoothly. Chips are easier to handle than money and can be stacked up and easily counted.

You should have at least two packs of new cards available. Use packs with different back designs, for example one blue pack and one red pack. Leave the cards sealed in their packets until they are needed for play. Allow the other players to examine the cards to check for marks. At regular intervals throughout a session of poker, you should use new cards. This helps cut down on the possibilities for cheating. If cards get marked, new cards can be used. Switching to a new pack with a different back design will ensure that if any cards have been stolen from the pack, they can't get used in the next game.

Ensure that you have enough players to make a game worthwhile. You should aim for a minimum of at least four players and no more than 10 players per table.

If there is going to be a lot of money on the premises, ensure that you have adequate security. There is a risk that you could get robbed. Keep doors locked. Also be alert when you leave a game, especially if you have won a lot of money.

It is customary for the host to provide refreshments for the players. Ideally, these should be provided during set breaks so that the game is not held up. You should provide something that is easy and quick to eat, like sandwiches or pizza. Take care to limit the amount of alcohol available. Do not drink too much yourself as it may affect your judgement when playing. Also try to limit the amount the other players drink as disputes can get out of hand if players are drunk.

Play should be organized in such a way that gives as little opportunity as possible for cheating. Draw lots to decide the seating arrangement. Change the seating arrangement after a break. Each player should take it in turns to shuffle and deal the cards. A player other than the dealer should cut the cards prior to dealing. Change the decks after a couple of hours. Mutually agree a time at which the game will end.

Strategies for playing

In a private game, you are likely to play with the same people each time. This gives you the opportunity to build up a detailed analysis of the way in which each person plays. You will be able to judge if they are loose or tight players. You will also have the time to analyse their body language and look for tells. Each time you play make notes. You can study these records and determine your future strategy.

Of course, the other players also have the opportunity to study *your* methods of play. You will need to vary your play to make it more difficult for them to guess your hand. After each game, assess your strategy. Try to identify weaknesses in your play. Does your body language give too much away? Should you use a different betting strategy? Are you staying in for too long on hands that should be folded? Do your attempts at bluffing fail? When you won a pot, could you have made it a bigger pot by using a different betting strategy?

You should adapt your strategy to take account of any changes in the rules. Bear in mind the implications of playing with wildcards as they make achieving the higher hands much easier.

12

playing in a casino

In this chapter you will learn:
- about playing poker in a casino
- about costs
- about entry requirements
- how play is organized
- etiquette.

Casinos

Casinos are purpose-built gaming establishments that offer facilities for playing a wide range of gambling games including various forms of poker. Casinos are legal in many countries and often state controlled or legislated. They tend to be located in resorts and large population areas. Local gaming laws determine when they may open. There are casinos in many countries around the world where poker can be played including Great Britain, United States of America, Canada, continental Europe, South Africa and Australia. Some casinos also give lessons in the games. These allow players to practise without risking any money. Casinos also host poker tournaments.

British casinos

Great Britain has over 130 casinos. They tend to be found in large towns and cities and in tourist areas. There are over 20 in London. More than 40 casinos have facilities for playing poker.

British casinos are strictly controlled by the Gaming Board who issue licences for premises and casinos staff. Checks are carried out to ensure that no gaming personnel or casino owners have criminal records. Daily opening hours are from 2.00pm to 4.00am.

All the casinos are member-only clubs. In order to gamble, you need to become a member or, alternatively, to be signed in by a member. You will be required to show two forms of identification, one of which must be a major form of identification such as a passport. After you have applied for membership, 24 hours must pass before you are allowed to gamble. Some casinos also charge a membership fee. If you are travelling from abroad and want to gamble, it is possible to apply for membership in advance.

Continental Europe

Most countries on continental Europe have casinos. They tend to be smaller, more intimate establishments than those found in the United States. Countries with casinos include Austria, Belgium, France, Germany, Greece, Monaco, the Netherlands. Poker is becoming more popular in Europe and is played in increasingly more casinos.

United States and Canadian casinos

Casino gaming is legal in most of the United States. The casinos are huge establishments and are often incorporated in larger leisure complexes. They are located in the traditional venues of Las Vegas and Atlantic City and also on Native American reservations. Most are open 24 hours a day. Over 260 casinos have facilities for poker.

In Canada, there are government-owned casinos, 24 of which offer poker. Resort casinos are located in tourist areas. There are also provincial casinos that attract locals.

The southern hemisphere

Australia has 14 casinos, one in each state and territory, which are privately operated under government-granted franchises. New Zealand has five casinos located in the major cities and Gold Coast resorts. Four casinos have facilities for poker. South Africa has over 30 casinos controlled by the National Gambling Board for South Africa.

Selecting a casino

The amount you have budgeted for will largely determine the sort of casino you frequent. The minimum stakes for betting can vary quite considerably in different casinos. Generally, the more upmarket the club, the higher the stakes will be. You will therefore need to consider how many chips of the minimum stake your budget will purchase and how long they will last.

If you are playing for high stakes you will have more choice and can look for the best facilities. The more upmarket casinos provide private rooms for games. This facility allows high-staking customers to play in quieter surroundings. Instead of paying a percentage of the pot, you can often negotiate an hourly rate for this service.

Playing in a casino

The casino provides all the facilities for playing poker including the gaming table, dealer and cards. There are set rules that determine how the game is dealt, how the betting is organized and what happens in the event of a dispute. A printed version of the rules is available on request.

Games played include Texas hold 'em, Omaha, seven-card stud, Caribbean stud poker and pai gow poker. The games are played with casino chips that can be purchased either on the gaming tables or from the cashpoint. When you leave the casino, you simply hand in your chips at the cashpoint where they will be redeemed for money.

How casino games vary from private games

Casino poker is more formal. The games are dealt in a fast and efficient manner.

There is a limited choice of games. The games tend to be restricted to those that give higher profits for casinos. Games such as five-card draw are rarely played as there are fewer betting rounds than games like texas hold 'em.

The rules of the game are written down and played in a standard way. Wildcards are not used.

The dealer is employed by the casino and does not play in the game.

Cheats are actively pursued and barred.

The competitors you will be playing against will be strangers.

Casinos offer both games where players play against each other for a pot, and banking games where the player plays against the casino.

Why gamble in a casino?

The main incentive is to win money. The potential winnings are unlimited. This is because there is always a supply of players with large bankrolls. In many casinos, it is also possible to play around the clock. There is always a game available. You will also gain more experience, as you will be playing against players of different abilities from beginners to professional gamblers.

One of the main advantages of playing in a casino is that you are guaranteed fairness. Chapter 8 describes some of the many ways of cheating at poker. In a casino, there are many controls in place to make the games fair. The dealer is employed by the casino so has no interest in the game. This eliminates all methods of cheating involved with dealing. New packs of cards are used and are constantly checked for marks. This rules out marked cards being used.

The casino staff allocates the seats, which makes it more difficult for colluding players to get on the same game. Players' winnings are monitored, which makes it easy to identify colluding players. All games are videotaped and can be played back to identify cheats. If cheats are caught, they are barred from the casino. Their details are also given to other casinos, which makes it difficult for them to play elsewhere.

A casino is a safe environment with security staff who will ensure that disputes are settled in a civil manner. You may win in a private game but here could find yourself having to return your winnings to a player who threatens you with physical violence.

Costs

Playing in a casino is more expensive than it is in a private game. The casino makes a charge for the use of its services. In poker games, this charge is in the form of a commission, usually a percentage of the pot. This charge is called the rake and is typically 10 per cent of the pot. Other casinos may charge an hourly rate for the use of their facilities. With Caribbean stud poker the charge is in the form of a house advantage. This means that winning bets are paid out at odds lower than the true chance of winning.

In some countries casino winnings are taxable. In the United States, for example, there is a 30 per cent tax on winnings. Non-resident aliens from some countries can apply for exemption. It is best to check the local legislation before betting as you could get a big shock when your tax bill arrives.

Some casinos also charge an entrance and membership fee.

Tipping the dealer

Check local customs about tipping. In Great Britain, it is illegal to tip gaming staff. In the United States and continental Europe it is customary, but not obligatory, to tip the dealer if you win the pot.

Entry requirements

Some form of identification such as a passport or driving licence will often need to be shown as proof of identity and age. Some casinos may require you to enrol as a member. This will involve filling in a form with personal details such as name and address. The minimum age for gambling is often the age of majority but can be older. In the USA, it is 21. In most other countries, it is 18.

Many casinos have a dress code. Generally, the more expensive establishments have stricter rules so it is advisable to wear smart dress. Often men are required to wear a tie and jacket.

You may be refused entry if you have been previously barred from a casino. This is because casinos share information about players caught cheating.

You are not allowed to take electronic items such as computers, calculators and cameras on the gaming floor. This is to prevent cheating.

Subliminal practices

Casinos use a number of subliminal practices to keep you on the premises for longer and to make you bet more. This includes gaming rooms where clocks and windows are absent, serving refreshments at the gaming tables and providing comp schemes. Comp is short for complimentary. Comp schemes allow players to accumulate points that can be redeemed against refreshments, hotel accommodation and entertainment tickets.

Chips are used instead of money. This makes it easy to get carried away and bet more than you intended, as you do not associate the chip with its true value.

Stakes

For each game, stakes will be advertised. At peak times, for instance weekends and holidays, the minimum stakes may be raised. Players need to ensure that they have enough chips to last a game, as they are not usually allowed to purchase more chips until a game is completed. A game of draw poker requires around 40 times the minimum stake. Seven-card stud requires around 50 times. Hold 'em and Omaha need around 100 times.

Players who run out of chips during a game can still have a chance of winning a proportion of the pot. This is called the all-in rule. When a player runs out of chips, a second pot is started. The other players continue to play, contributing to the second pot. The winner of the game gets the second pot. The hand of the winner is then compared with that of the player who ran out of money. The player with the highest ranking hand wins the first pot.

How play is organized

Poker is often played in a separate room, usually referred to as the card room. There will be a number of tables offering different games at different stake levels. Around eight to 10 players can be seated at a table.

To start playing, you need to register for a game. If there is a seat free, you will be able to start playing immediately. If all the seats are occupied, your name will be entered on a list and called out when a place is available.

In order to play, you will need to purchase chips. These are usually plastic discs and plaques marked with an equivalent amount of money. The chips can be purchased from the cashpoint and from gaming tables. You need to ensure that you purchase enough chips to complete a game of poker as you will often not be allowed to purchase more chips midway through a game. The game played will determine how many chips you need. As a general guide, seven-card stud needs about 50 times the minimum stake. Hold 'em and Omaha need about 100 times the minimum stake. If you play hold 'em with a minimum stake of £2, you will need to have £200 worth of chips.

Each table is operated by a casino dealer, who is responsible for running the game. The dealer will shuffle and deal the cards, exchange money for chips, check that the players have bet the correct amount, place players bets into the pot, remove losing hands, give change and pay the pot to the winner. The dealer also ensures the players are not cheating.

Card room etiquette

Each card room will have a set of rules about how players are expected to behave at the table. Most of the rules are designed to combat cheating.

The following is a general guide:

- Players may only touch their own cards and chips.
- All cards must remain in view at all times. They can't, for example, be held under the table or in a player's pocket.
- If a player drops a card or reveals one to another player, the hand is declared dead. The player will not be allowed to participate with the hand and any money contributed to the pot will be lost.
- Placing a chip on top of your cards shows you are still in the game.
- Chips must never be thrown.
- Bets must not be put directly into the pot. A bet is made by placing sufficient chips in front of you. The dealer checks that the amount is correct and adds them to the pot. This ensures that no one bets light.
- Players must give clear verbal instructions of their action. By calling out 'time', they will be granted extra time to make a decision.
- Players may stop playing when they like. They may also take breaks. If you intend to return to the game, you may leave your chips on the table. The dealer will ensure they are not touched. However, if you are absent for a long period, your seat may be allocated to another player.
- Don't put drinks directly on the gaming table as they disrupt the game if spilt. You will be provided either with a drinks holder or a separate table.

Banking games

Banking games like Caribbean stud poker and pai gow poker are usually played on tables located in the main gaming room. They are much faster games than that played for a pot. The dealer will exchange cash for chips, deal the cards, check that the correct stakes are bet and payout the winning bets.

Fairness of the game

Strict controls are in place to ensure that players get a fair deal. In most countries, government legislation and agencies ensure that games pay out a fair return to the players and that gaming equipment is fair. Casino staff, operators and premises are often licensed. Any infringement of gaming legislation can lead to their licence being withdrawn.

Gaming equipment is precision made and thoroughly checked before use. New packs of cards are used. At the beginning of gaming, the playing cards are laid out on the table to show that full decks are being used. The cards are also scrutinized to check for any marks that could give players an unfair advantage. Any creased or marked cards are removed and replaced. While gaming is in progress, the cards are continually scrutinized and any that become marked are removed and replaced. At the end of gaming, the old cards are counted to ensure that none have been removed. They are then discarded.

The way that the cards are shuffled in a casino ensures that they are thoroughly mixed. A combination of methods is used including face down mixing, riffle shuffling and cutting of the cards. Usually, a player is invited to insert a blank card into the pack to cut them.

As well as the dealer, a number of other casino staff watch the games to ensure there is no cheating. An inspector checks the work of the dealer and is responsible for looking for cheats. The inspector also resolves any disputes that may arise. Since the games are recorded on videotape disputes are easily settled. If you encounter a problem or suspect another player of cheating, ask the dealer to call the inspector. The pit boss is in charge of a group of tables and will often watch the games, again to ensure fair play. Security staff also carry out surveillance of players. Some wear uniforms and others are plain clothed and not obvious.

In addition to checking the videotapes of the game, the winning records of players can also be analysed. Players who are consistently winning will be more closely watched for signs of cheating.

Casino records

Casinos keep records of how much players win and lose. They use this information to identify cheats and allocate comps. This information may also be passed to government agencies for the purposes of taxation and controlling money laundering. In the USA, for example, personal details of players winning large amounts are given to the IRS.

Comps

Comps is short for complimentary and the term refers to free refreshments, cigarettes, hotel rooms, flights and show tickets. A player's level of spending will determine the type of comps they receive and how many. Some casinos operate a comp scheme where players can enrol to collect points towards comps. Players with large bankrolls are called high rollers or whales and receive all the comps going.

13

playing on the internet

In this chapter you will learn:
- about the history of internet poker
- how to play
- how to play safely
- playing strategies.

What is internet poker?

Internet poker, also referred to as online poker, is playing poker via a computer connection over the internet. Internet poker firms supply computer software via their websites to connect players from all over the world so that they compete against one another in a game of poker. The games can be played 24 hours a day, seven days a week in the privacy of the players' own homes.

All types of poker can be played. Online card rooms offer a variety of games including Texas hold'em, five-card draw, seven-card stud and Omaha. You can play in live games for money or in free games for fun. There are games at all stake levels starting from £0.01 to no-limit games where you can bet as much as you like. You can also watch games in progress. A wide choice of tournaments is also offered.

For real-money games, a rake of typically 5 per cent is charged for the use of the poker room services. The rake is deducted from the winning pot. The rake charged varies with different poker sites. Some offer reduced rates for regular customers. Others may take no rake if, for example, you fold before the flop on texas hold 'em.

In addition to card rooms, there are internet casinos. These offer poker banking games like Caribbean stud poker and pai gow poker and video poker games like jacks or better, deuces wild and joker wild. Here, similar conditions exist as in traditional casinos with the house building in an advantage to the fixed odds. Instead of paying out winnings at the true odds, lower odds are paid to allow the casino to make a profit.

The history of internet poker

The first online card room was introduced by Planet Poker in 1998. A year later Paradise Poker arrived and became the industry leader. Their prominent position was overtaken by Party Poker owned by PartyGaming. It is now the world's largest poker room with over 50 per cent of the online poker market. The site was launched in 2001. It is licensed and regulated by the government of Gibraltar and has over 70,000 simultaneous players and 8000 tables during peak traffic time each day. It annually hosts the PartyPoker.com Million, an offline tournament with over £7 million in prizes.

The popularity of online poker is growing year on year. In 2003 there were an estimated 600,000 people playing online. Now it is estimated that over 1.2 million people play internet poker.

Is internet poker legal?

Depending on where you live, internet betting may or may not be legal. In many countries, legislation has yet to catch up with the phenomenon of internet gambling. Much gambling legislation is outdated. As the legal situation may change at any time, you are advised to check the legality of internet betting in your jurisdiction before placing any bets.

In the UK, it is legal to play and bet on internet poker. The Gambling Act 2005 legislates remote betting. Remote betting includes all types of betting where the parties involved in a bet are not face to face. This includes betting over the internet, telephone and future technology that may arise, such as betting via your television. The Gambling Act 2005 replaces most of the existing law about gambling in Great Britain. A new organisation, the Gambling Commission, was formally established on 1st Ocotober 2005 and is responsible for controlling gambling by regulating and licensing operators. Licensed gaming sites on the internet carry a kitemark to show that the necessary standards have been met.

In Australia, the Interactive Gambling Act of 2001 prohibits operators from providing online gambling services. In most cases, it is legal for individuals to gamble online.

In the United States, the situation is less clear. The Wire Act is often cited as the appropriate legislation covering internet betting but this specifically deals with operating a sports betting business. Case law appears to show that online gambling is legal but the US Justice Department insists otherwise. In November 2004 Antigua and Barbuda won a World Trade Organization ruling that United States legislation criminalizing internet betting violates global laws.

If you live in an area where internet poker is not legal, you may find it impossible to get an online card room to accept bets from you.

Why play internet poker?

Internet poker allows you the convenience of playing in your own home at a time that suits you. There is always a game on no matter what time of the day or night. Many people find playing on the internet less intimidating than playing in a casino. They can remain anonymous to the other players. They are identified only by their pseudonyms. There is no need to worry about having a poker face.

Internet poker can work out cheaper than going to a bricks and mortar casino. The rake in an internet casino is just 5 per cent, which is lower than many casinos. In addition, you don't have to pay membership fees or travel costs. You also do not have to worry about a dress code. Via the internet you can play in your pyjamas and no one will know.

There is a huge amount of competition for customers, which means tax-free betting, low commission rates, initial free bets and bonuses are all offered. It is therefore worth shopping around to find a good deal.

How fair is internet poker?

Some governments strictly regulate online gambling. In the UK, for example, checks are made into the background of the firm's owners to ensure that they are fit and proper persons. They must demonstrate that they have sufficient funds to pay out to players. Software used must be audited to ensure that it is fair. Players' money must be 'ringfenced' so that it is protected and cannot be used by the firm for running expenses etc. They are required to run responsible gambling sites carrying details of where problem gamblers can get help.

Cheating

Combating cheating has always been a priority for online poker firms. Online poker is vulnerable to *collusion*. With online poker because you can't see the other players, you can communicate your hand to another player. It is easy for two players who are friends to communicate while playing either over the phone or via instant messaging. If the two decide to collude, whichever player has the better hand plays his hand, while the other folds. This way they have two chances of getting a better hand. If more players cooperate as a team, the victim stands little chance of winning.

It would also be possible for a computer expert to operate a number of computers consecutively and make it appear that several players are competing against one another when in fact all the computers are in one room and he is controlling the action of all the players bar one in a game. In this situation, as he knows all the hands except that of one opponent, he can play in such a way that the highest ranking hand always wins.

The online poker rooms are aware of this form of cheating and combat it using software to detect colluders. The software monitors the frequency of two players playing in the same game, unusually high winning rates and suspicious playing patterns, like players folding when they have very good hands. If colluders are caught they will have their accounts suspended and may lose any money held in their accounts. Their membership to the poker room will be cancelled and details of their cheating may be shared with other gambling sites, which will make it more difficult for them to open another account with a poker room. If you suspect that this kind of cheating has occurred in a game that you have been involved in, you should inform the site.

How internet poker works

The online card rooms use computer software to produce virtual card rooms. Players see a depiction of a card table on their screen, showing the other players (cartoon style) and details of their own hand much like you see on console games.

The software uses a random number generator to determine the order of the deck of cards. This ensures that with each game, the cards are randomly shuffled. The software deals the cards and prompts the players to make their decisions about their hands. At the appropriate times in the games, it gives the options of check, call, bet, raise or fold. These options will appear on the screen. Players select which option they want by clicking with their computer mouse. The screen will tell you how much you need to bet to stay in the game and provide the options that you have at that point in the game. Throughout the game, a running total of the pot and the actions of the other players are shown. At the showdown, the cards of the remaining players will be revealed. The software deducts the amount of the bets from the players' account and credits any winning pots to their account.

Because the games are operated by a computer they are run at a much faster pace than normal poker games. There is no dealer, so there is no time wasted while cards are shuffled, dealt and collected. There is often a time limit imposed. If you do not act within the time limit, then your hand is folded.

The rules tend to be similar to those found in bricks and mortar casinos. Due to the internet environment, there are also special rules that cover what happens if a player gets cut off from the internet during a game (see later).

Cards are burnt as in a normal poker game. You don't see the cards getting burnt. The players take it in turn to be the dealer. They don't physically deal the cards themselves. All the dealing is carried out by the software. A disc (dealer button) will indicate which player is the current dealer.

Once all the cards are dealt, the various options that are available during the game will appear on the screen – raise, call, check and fold. The first player has one of three choices, check, bet or fold. Once a bet has been placed, the subsequent players must call, raise or fold. In draw poker, you will need to select the cards you want to hold.

Players can take a break, leaving the game for a short while and returning to the same table.

Before you play

You will need a computer with an internet connection. The faster your connection the better as delays in transmission of data can slow down games. With time limits placed on betting, you will need to ensure that your computer quickly communicates your decision.

You will need to find a suitable online card room or casino. The website addresses of major poker sites are given at the end of the book (see taking it further, page 174). Before you can play, you will need to sign up for an account with an internet card room. This involves filling in an online form with your personal details. The general requirements are that you are over 18 years of age and live in a place where internet betting is legal. In some countries, you may need to be older. Proof of your age and residence may be required. You will need to ensure that you comply with your own local, national or state laws before opening an account or placing a bet. If you live in an area where internet gambling is illegal, you may be refused an account.

Registration involves selecting a user name and password that you will need to log on to the site. The user name will usually be a nickname that will identify you when you play. You should keep your password secret to stop other people logging on to your account and placing bets. You will need an email address so that you can be contacted by the internet firm. Accounts are often available in a choice of currencies so that you will be able to bet in your local currency.

Downloading and installing software

Before you start playing you will need to download and then install software on your computer. The software will run the game programs.

A site will typically list the minimum system requirements needed to play their software:

- the version of Windows that is supported
- download size – how much space you need on your hard disk to install the software and how quickly this will download
- amount of RAM required
- minimum requirements for your modem.

The software keeps records of the hands that have been played. You can look at your hand history. This gives you the opportunity to analyse your game and see where you are going wrong.

Depositing and withdrawing money

In order to start betting, you will first need to deposit money with the card room. Money can be deposited in various ways including credit cards, debit cards, cheques, money orders etc. For speed, credit cards and debit cards are ideal. They allow you to directly deposit funds and immediately start betting.

You can withdraw your money in a number of ways. With some sites, your money will be credited back to the source of the money. So, for example, if you deposited money from a credit card, a withdrawal of money will be credited to your credit card account.

Joining a game

To begin playing, you will need to log on to your account. This will take you to the lobby. Here you will find a list of all the games currently in progress. If there is an empty seat at a table you click on 'Join game' and you will be taken to that game. If there are no empty seats available, you can put your name on a waiting list. You can specify what stakes you want to play for and how many people you want to play against.

For each table there will be details of how many players are currently sitting at the table and how many are on the waiting list. If you put your name on the waiting list, you will be notified when a place becomes available.

You can sit in any chair that is available. You will be shown the player's nicknames and how much money they are playing with.

An information box will tell you the name of the game, the limits and type of game the blinds, ante and the buy-in.

When you first sit down at a table, you are prompted to enter the amount of your buy-in. There will be a minimum buy-in, which will depend on the game being played.

Take your time to familiarize yourself with the layout as they differ with different sites. Most sites allow you to customize the screen to suit your taste.

Watch the games before playing and only join once you are confident that you understand exactly what you need to do. Read the terms and conditions before agreeing to them. Many sites have a code of conduct.

What happens if you get disconnected from the internet

If you get disconnected from the internet while a game is in progress, the way that your hand is treated will vary with different sites, so you should carefully check the rules. In general, your hand will automatically be played as all in. If check is an option, the system will check for you. If not, you will go all in and a separate pot will be created. If you have the winning hand, then you will be awarded the pot that built up at the time that you were disconnected. To avoid abuse of this feature, players are limited to a number of all ins in a 24-hour period. If you exceed the number of all ins in that time, your hand will be automatically folded if you get cut off from the internet.

Chatting to other players

Players can chat to each other during play by typing messages from their keyboards. There are restrictions on what you can say. It is forbidden to talk about what is in your hand during a game. Even after you have folded, you must not tell other players what you had in your hand until the game is completed. Giving away information about your hand during a game helps the other players to make decisions. You may chat freely once a game has finished. To save time and typing out long sentences, abbreviations are used while chatting. Some of the abbreviation used are shown below. Offensive language is not allowed. Writing in capitals or using exclamation marks makes you appear to be shouting.

Chat terms

brb – be right back

gg – good game

gh – good hand

gp – good play

gtg – got to go

hehe – very amusing

lol – laugh out loud

nh – nice hand

omg – oh my god

tx – thanks

ty – thank you

wb – welcome back

wp – well played

wtg – way to go

vnh – very nice hand

Playing safe

Care needs to be taken when gambling on the internet as there are many unregulated sites in foreign juridstictions. Some governments have introduced strict controls for sites operating in their countries.

Although internet betting offers greater convenience to the customer, it does need to be treated with caution as there are a number of scam sites and sites that have gone bust owing customers money. Betting on the internet is a relatively new phenomenon and there is a lack of control and legal framework to deal with problems that may arise. Be extremely cautious of betting with unregulated sites in foreign jurisdictions. If a site goes bust, it will be virtually impossible for you to get your money back.

The internet is a highly competitive business environment and many businesses have been trading for a relatively short time. Check that a site is authorized to operate in the country where you are living. If you place bets and the site is subsequently closed down you may lose your money.

Ideally, you should look for a site that is government regulated. Look for a site that has a good reputation. You need to ensure that your money is protected and that the games are fair. A card room should have its card-shuffling software independently audited to check that it is fair.

Ensure that the site actively checks for colluders and has a policy of barring anyone caught. Also look for a company that has a policy of limiting the number of all ins. This will stop cheats taking advantage of the all-in rule. Before you deposit money with a company, check it out thoroughly. There are lots of gambling forums on the internet where gamblers discuss their experiences about online poker. There are also many sites that give blacklists of companies that have failed to pay out or to treat customers fairly.

Look for a site that gives 24-hour support, seven days a week. This ensures that if you have any problems you can contact a member of staff no matter what time of day it is.

Keep your password secret. Anyone who has access to your password could place bets and withdraw money from your bank account or credit card. If you use a computer that is accessible by more than one person, don't save the password so that it can be automatically entered by the computer. Another person using the computer would be able to access your account.

Ensure you use a site where personal information is encrypted. As you may be giving personal details, bank account information and credit card numbers to a site, you will want to be sure that this information is securely transmitted and safely held so that it cannot be accessed by a third party.

Phishing

Phishing is a method used to obtain a players password to their online poker account. What will generally happen is that the victim will get an email claiming to be from customer support from the poker site. They will give some spurious reason why the customer needs to contact them. The victim will be directed to a web page where it will be necessary to type in his user name and password. The cheater then has the information needed to log on to the victim's account and bet with the money in the account. The cheater then bets all the victim's money on a hand where he is head to head with him and all the money from the victim's account is transferred to his own.

Government agencies and poker sites are actively working to combat this fraud. The poker site will often quickly be aware that a fraud of this type is being attempted and will send a warning to members or post a warning on its site. If you get an email claiming to be from the poker site, do not click on any of the links posted in the email. Instead, go directly to the site and log on from the site's home page. If you suspect that you have received a phishing email report it directly to the site.

All-in abuse

Some players will abuse the all-in rule. They will disconnect their computer at a time when it is advantageous to do so. To combat this, sites place limits on the number of times that all in can be used. If the player is disconnected again, then their hand is automatically folded.

Disputes with internet poker sites

If a site is government licensed, you can address any complaints about the site to the licensing authority.

If a firm is a member of the Interactive Gaming Council (IGC), it is possible to apply to the IGC for mediation if you have a complaint against a member company.

GamCare certification

GamCare is a registered charity that is the UK's national centre for information, advice and practical help regarding the social impact of gambling. It gives certification to businesses that implement the GamCare Code of Practice for Remote Gambling, which involves implementing the following practices:

- age verification systems
- controls for customer spend
- reality checks within game screens
- self-exclusion options for players
- information about responsible gambling and sources of advice and support
- social responsibility content and sources
- training for customer services in problem gambling and social responsibility.

Details of accredited companies are available on the GamCare website.

Playing strategy

There is no physical contact between the players. You cannot see them and they cannot see you. This means you do not have to worry about keeping a poker face and paying attention to your body language. This also means that you cannot assess other players' body language and look for tells. As technology improves games may be introduced where the players can see each other via web cameras.

As you cannot see the players, you need to develop a different strategy for playing. The strategy used needs to be based more on probabilities, betting patterns and knowledge gained from previous games with players whom you may encounter in the future. If you regularly play on the same site, you may regularly play with the same players and build up a body of information about the habits and betting patterns of these players.

14

tournament play

In this chapter you will learn:
- about types of tournaments
- about the major tournaments
- playing tips.

Poker tournaments

A poker tournament is a competition between players for prizes. Competing in tournaments is an increasingly popular way to play poker. Each year more and more tournaments are being organized. They give players the opportunity to win a large prize for a relatively small entry fee instead of placing bets. The more prestigious events attract players with greater skill and pay bigger prizes. For less experienced players, there are many tournaments at lower stake levels.

Tournaments can be played at casinos, card rooms and on the internet. Casinos tend to hold tournaments at off-peak times. There are tournaments for all different types of poker game, including Texas hold 'em, seven-card stud and Omaha. Hold 'em is the most common tournament game, as it was chosen to decide the champion in the World Series of Poker.

Tournaments allow players to test their skill against a large field of competitors. A minor tournament may have several hundred competitors. Major tournaments attract several thousand players. This gives players a great deal of experience. You will encounter competitors at various levels of skill ranging from hopeless to highly accomplished.

An advantage of tournaments is that they can work out a much cheaper way of playing than regular casino play, particularly in the minor tournaments. Assuming you get through the initial rounds, an entire day's play can cost a fraction of the price of a regular game. You know in advance how much it will cost. You also have a rough idea of the potential prizes.

Tournament play requires stamina and concentration. With conventional games, you can take a break when you like and quit when you are ahead. With tournament play you are there for the duration, which can be up to 14 hours or more in one day. There are allotted breaks but they are short. A typical tournament will allow an hour for lunch and 10-minute breaks every $1^{1}/_{2}$–2 hours. In the World Series of Poker, for example most events last two days. On the first day play starts at noon and continues until the competitors win their place for the final table. On the second day the finalists start playing at 4pm and continue until one wins.

Types of tournament

There are two main types of tournament – freeze-out or no re-buy tournaments and re-buy tournaments. In both types of game players are eliminated when they lose all their chips.

Freeze-out/no re-buy tournaments

A freeze out tournament (no re-buy) is where each player receives an equal amount of chips at the start of the game. For example, an entry fee of £50 is paid and each player receives 500 chips. They play with this fixed amount of chips until the end of the game. If they get low on chips, they are not allowed to buy more. Players who lose all their chips are eliminated. If there is a time limit, the winner is the player with the most chips at the end of the competition. In other tournaments, play may continue until there is one winner at each table (all the other players have been eliminated). The winner then competes in the next round. Depending on the number of competitors, there may be several rounds to gradually eliminate players. Breaks are allotted to allow players time to relax and eat. After each round of play, seats are reallocated for the next level. This may be by further draw or may be determined in advance: for example, the finalists of table 1 may be scheduled to play the finalists of table 2.

Re-buy tournaments

In re-buy tournaments players are allowed to purchase extra chips at set points during the game. The amount of the re-buys is usually the same as the initial buy-in. In some tournaments, re-buying of chips is unlimited. In others, there are limits. The rules may stipulate, for example, that there are two further re-buys allowed. Play continues until players have no remaining chips or for a time limit where the player with the most chips is declared the winner.

Progressive stack re-buy tournaments

In progressive stack re-buy games, the cost of the re-buy remains constant but the further you are into the re-buy period, the more chips you get. The effect of this is that the value of the chips decreases as the game continues.

Pot limit and no pot limit

There are two terms that refer to the size of the bets. They are pot limit and no pot limit. A pot limit is where the size of the bets may be any amount between that of the big blind (initial bet in Texas hold 'em) and the total pot. A no pot limit means bets may be of any amount between the value of the big blind and the value of your remaining chips.

Costs

The costs for entering a tournament comprise the buy-in, re-buys and an entry fee. Minimum buy-ins start from around £15 to £20 and pay prizes of several hundred dollars. Buy-ins for major tournaments are as much as £10,000 with prizes of £1.5 million. The entry fee is kept by the casino to cover the cost of operating the tournament. An entry fee is typically 10 per cent of the buy-in.

To find the overall cost of a tournament, you will need to total the buy-in, cost of any re-buys and the entry fee. For example, a tournament advertised with a buy in of £1000 and an entry fee of £100, will cost £1100 in total. A tournament advertised with a £500 buy-in and a £50 entry fee with two re-buys of £500 would cost a total of £1550 if you participate in all the buy-ins.

Entry requirements

Players are required to fill in a registration form and may be asked for proof of age and identity. Players must be over the minimum age to gamble. This varies depending on local gambling legislation. It is often the age of majority but can be older. Many tournaments are oversubscribed so it is advisable to register early. At the registration, players pay the amount of the buy-in. If you pay the buy-in by cheque, ensure you register early enough for the cheque to clear.

Some major tournaments have particular entry requirements. Players may be required to have won or have been placed in a major tournament. Alternatively, a player may have to compete in a qualifying competition to gain entry. Most tournaments also have separate competitions for women players.

How play is organized

The tournament will be advertised giving the major conditions, such as the amount of the buy-in, the value and number of re-buys and entry fee. A set of rules will be available. Play will be scheduled to take place over a certain amount of time. Some tournaments last for a few hours; others can be as long as several days.

A random draw is usually held to allocate seats. Players should take up their seats when directed to do so. It is advisable to arrive at least half an hour before play starts. If you do not arrive on time, your seat may be allocated to another player or, alternatively, you may be disqualified.

The casino will supply a dealer who will control the game. The dealer will initially check that the correct players are seated at the table. The competition starts with an announcement of shuffle up and deal. The dealer will give the players their chips. Other casino staff will watch the game to ensure it is fairly played.

Each tournament will have its own set of rules. Commonly, players are not allowed to converse either with each other or the spectators. Players must make all their own decisions and are not allowed to ask spectators or other players for advice. Players are not allowed to lend or borrow chips.

If a player runs out of chips during a hand, the all-in rule usually applies. This means that the players can still win the pot to which they have contributed. A second pot is then started for further bets.

The games will be closely watched for cheats who, if caught, will be disqualified. Games are usually videotaped and can be played back in the event of a dispute. The chances of players colluding are reduced as a random draw decides where players sit.

Prizes

At the end of play there will usually be a short ceremony to present the prizes. They are mostly paid out in cash. In some tournaments, the prize can be the entry fee to enter a major competition (see satellites). As well as the prize for the winner, there will often be prizes for several runners-up.

The prizes for most tournaments will depend on how many competitors there are. The value of all the buy-ins is totalled to give the prize money. In tournaments where re-buys are allowed, the value of the re-buys is also contributed to the prize money. The casino will often make a deduction for the rake (charge for playing). The majority of the prize fund is awarded to the winner. Several runners-up share the remainder. Some tournaments are winner takes all. In some tournaments, there will be a guaranteed minimum prize. Often the prize will be more than the minimum. In British tournaments, the entire buy-in must be returned as prize money and no additional entry fee can be charged.

Satellites

A satellite is a poker tournament that allows a player to win the stake to compete in a major tournament. For the major tournaments, the minimum stake for the final is high. For example, it may cost £10,000 to enter a tournament. A satellite may be organized for 10 players with a £1000 buy-in. Play continues until there is only one player remaining. The winner receives all the stake money, that is £10,000, which is enough to enter the main tournament.

For an even smaller stake, players can enter a super satellite. If they win it will also give them enough money to buy a seat in the major tournament. In super satellites, there is more competition. Players may have to compete in several levels of play to win the stake for the major tournament. In the World Series of Poker, for example, there are super satellites costing £220, which give the players the opportunity of winning the £10,000 needed to enter the major competition.

Some major tournaments also organize satellites in different countries and on the internet. The prize will often include flights and hotel accommodation. (See World Heads-up Poker Championship on page 151).

UK competitions

In the UK, the Gaming Board provides guidelines for the running of card room competitions. Details of all fees, rules and names and stakes of the players must be prominently displayed in the card room. Players must receive a receipt for entry stakes, registration fees and re-buys. All entry stakes and re-buys must be returned to winning players as prize money. The casino may also add money to the prize. A competition registration fee may be charged in addition to the entry stakes. This fee may not be greater than 10 per cent of the entry stake and may be no greater than £50. Winners must sign a receipt for their prize. Re-buys are only allowed when the value of chips remaining in front of the player reaches 50 per cent of the chip value issued in exchange for the original entry stake. At the casino's discretion, a maximum of one 'top-up' re-buy may be issued to each player at the end of the re-buy period, regardless of the value of chips remaining in front of him.

If a competition is a satellite qualifier, it must be made clear whether or not travel and accommodation expenses are to be paid as part of the prize. If a player wins a satellite qualifier and travel and accommodation expenses are part of the prize, they are not required to enter the further competition. So, for example, if you win a flight and hotel accommodation as part of a prize you may go on the flight and stay in the accommodation without having to enter the next competition. If you do not enter the competition, you may be expected to forfeit the entry stake to the further competition.

Internet tournaments

The online card rooms offer vast numbers of poker tournaments. Internet tournaments are much shorter than traditional tournaments.

Single-table tournaments are where nine players compete. There is usually a prize for the top three finishers with the prize being divided as follows:

> winner 50%
> second place 30%
> third place 20%.

In multi-table tournaments, you will compete against hundreds of other players. The players will be on randomly located seats and may play several rounds. As players get knocked out, the remaining players are re-seated until just nine players remain on the final table. The winner is the player who wins all the other players' chips. The advantage of multi-table tournaments is that you can win a large prize for a small entry fee.

Speed tournaments

With speed tournaments the value of the blind increases every few minutes. This ensures that the tournament is quickly finished. Speed tournaments can be played both as single table games and multi-table games.

Major tournaments

World Series of Poker

The World Series of Poker is the biggest and longest running poker tournament in the world. It attracts the elite of poker players. It is held annually in May at Binion's Horseshoe Casino in Las Vegas. Across 30 days a variety of tournaments are held. Most games take place over two days, with play lasting for up to 14 hours in a day. Single table satellites are held 24 hours a day with buy-ins ranging from $170–$1015. Super satellites start from $220. The action culminates in the no-limit texas hold 'em tournament that takes place over four days. The entry fee is $10,000. The first prize is $1.5 million and membership of the Poker Hall of Fame. The finale is televised around the world.

Jack Binion World Open

The Jack Binion World Open is modelled on the World Series of Poker. It takes place at Binion's Horseshoe and in Gold Strike casinos in Tunica. It is held annually in March and April. Buy-ins start from $330 rising to $5100, for the main competition, which is a no-limit Texas hold 'em tournament. Over 3000 competitors enter the tournament. Satellites and super satellites with buy-ins from $120 allow players to win their entrance fee for the main tournament.

Tournament of Champions of Poker

The Tournament of Champions of Poker as the name suggests is for players who have won major poker tournaments. Entry is also possible by winning a qualifying event. It is held in July at the Orleans Hotel in Las Vegas. It comprises £500 buy-in one-day tournaments with a top prize of over £1 million.

European Championship

The European Championship is held at Casino Baden in Austria during October. The game played is seven-card stud. Over 450 players from 23 countries compete for a prize of over £550,000.

World Heads-up Poker Championship

This is held annually during May and June at the Concord Card Casino in Vienna, in Austria. The casino has Europe's largest card room with 30 tables and a tournament room with 20 tables. Poker is played 24 hours a day. The main event is no-limit hold 'em with a €640,000 purse. A seat in the main draw costs €2125. The winner's prize is €250,000. Satellites are played in card rooms throughout Europe, America and Australia. It is also possible to play satellites on the internet. Winners of satellites get a seat in the championship, a flight and hotel accommodation.

World Series of poker trial

During March the World Series of Poker trial is held at the Concord Card Casino in Vienna, in Austria. It duplicates the World Series of Poker held in Las Vegas with a no-limit Texas hold 'em competition that lasts four days.

Ladbrokes Poker Million Tournament

The Ladbrokes Poker Million Tournament is a televised tournament that takes place in Great Britain and the Isle of Man during August. Players compete for a £1 million first prize.

Crown Australian Poker Championship

The Crown Australian Poker Championship is also known as the Aussie Millions. The tournament is held at the Crown Casino in Melbourne during January. It is a winner takes all no limit hold 'em tournament with an entry fee of AU$10,000 and a AU$1 million first prize.

PartyPoker.com Million

The PartyPoker.com Million is a limit hold 'em tournament that takes place on a cruise ship. The prize pool is around £10 million.

Playing tips

If you are used to playing in private games, familiarize yourself with casino play. This may differ enormously to the games you are used to playing. Private games tend to be played with wildcards and hands that are not in the official ranking. Learn how the games are played and how the betting is organized in a casino.

Watch lots of tournaments before you start competing. You'll have more confidence if you are familiar with what is going on. Watch the strategy that each player is using and assess its effectiveness. Make notes. It will help you later to remember good strategies.

Make sure you fully understand the rules and the strategy for the tournament game before you play. Get a copy of the tournament rules and study them carefully.

Ensure that you understand all the jargon associated with poker tournaments. Lots of unfamiliar terms and slang words are used in poker (see glossary). If you don't understand a word being used, ask the casino staff for an explanation.

Practise the game as much as possible. This doesn't have to cost you any money. You can do this at home. You can also organize private games with your friends along the lines of tournament games.

Compete in minor tournaments and gradually work your way up before taking on the professionals. Don't start with major tournaments, as the competition will be the best of the world.

Make sure you have plenty of sleep and are well relaxed before a tournament. During the tournament, you will have to concentrate for around 10–12 hours at a stretch, which is very tiring. The breaks are extremely short, typically 10 minutes per $1^1/_2$ to 2 hours. During the break, get some fresh air and stretch your legs.

Avoid drinking alcohol as it slows down your reactions.

Keep a diary of your hands and how you and your competitors played. Analyse your games and how you played. This way you can learn from your mistakes. A diary can be particularly helpful if you play regularly in tournaments. You will often meet the same opponents in future competitions. By keeping a log of their strengths and weaknesses, you can improve your chances of beating them.

Aim to win the top prize. Don't sit back and relax when you know you've reached the prize level. A minor prize will be little more than your original stake.

Take advantage of the fact that you are playing against strangers. In your local card room you may not be the best player and your reputation may not intimidate other players. Your best friend may recognize the signs that you are bluffing. However, your competitors in the tournament will know nothing about your method of play or past blunders.

Don't be intimidated by your competitors. They may try to unnerve you by staring hard into your face. Learn to deal with such tactics. You may be up against strong competition with seasoned players who have won major tournaments but each game is different. Play to the best of your ability. It may just be enough to win.

Learn to quickly assess the other players. Look for their strengths and weaknesses. Even when you're not contending for the pot, closely watch how the other competitors are playing. Be prepared to revise your initial assessments.

Once you identify weak opponents, play aggressively against them. If your game finishes earlier than others, watch the competition. You may gain valuable information about your competitors in the next round.

Don't waste chips. To stay in a game it is important to save your chips for your best plays. Staying in for one extra round of betting unnecessarily will cost you a lot of chips. If you have a poor hand and don't intend to bluff, fold it early.

Take advantage of buy-ins. Having more chips allows you to attack more and play aggressively. Being constantly worried about your chip level will make you more cautious.

If buy-ins of chips are allowed during the game, some players deliberately try to lose chips to participate in the buy-in. If you play aggressively at this time, you can easily accumulate their chips. Your own chip level will also determine whether it is worth losing chips to participate in a buy-in.

Adapt your play to suit each stage of the game. Play aggressively in the early stages to accumulate chips and intimidate the other players. Some players will be nervous. By appearing confident and intimidating them with aggressive play, you can push them out of a game.

It is possible to bluff more than usual. This is because players tend to be more cautious and fold more easily in tournaments. Your assessment of the players will give you a good indication of when to bluff.

Once you are in a comfortable position with a lot of chips, play more tightly. Save your attacks for your best hands. Let the other players battle among one another.

Attack players who are low on chips. They are more likely to fold to stay in the game.

Don't attack aggressive players. Battling with an aggressive player can cost you a lot of chips. Wait until they have folded, then concentrate on attacking the other players.

Learn to adapt your play to suit the game. If there are several aggressive players at the beginning of the game let them knock each other out. Once most of the competition has been eliminated you can start to attack.

Don't get overconfident. You may be lucky with the draw and have poor competition on the first round but, as you progress to each new level in the tournament, the competition will get tougher.

If playing abroad, check the local tax laws. In, for example, the United States non-resident aliens are taxed 30 per cent on gross winnings. Residents of some countries including some of the EU and South Africa can claim exemption by completing IRS form 1001.

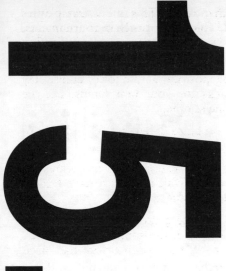

15

poker dice

In this chapter you will learn:
- how to play
- ranking of throws
- about keeping score.

Dice can also be used to play poker. This game is often called liar's dice. Five dice are used. The faces of each dice are marked like playing cards with an ace, king, queen, jack, 10 and 9. Although the game can be played with two players, it is more practical when played with between three and six players.

figure 15.1 symbols on the faces of the dice

How to play

The game is played with a cup/hat that covers the dice and that sits on a felt-covered saucer. The equipment allows each player in turn to look at the dice without revealing them to the other players. The players can wrap their hands around the cup and saucer and lift the cup just enough to see the throws without the other players seeing the dice. The five dice are used to make poker hands in a similar way to card games. The dice are thrown and the value of the upper-most face counts towards a poker hand.

figure 15.2 equipment for playing poker dice

The dice are ranked in the following descending order: ace, king, queen, jack, 10 and 9. The throws are ranked in the following descending order:

> five of a kind
> four of a kind
> full house
> high straight/big street
> low straight/small street
> three of a kind
> two pair
> one pair.

Five of a kind is five dice of the same value in the following descending order: five aces, five kings, five queens, five jacks, five tens or five nines. Therefore, five of a kind with kings will beat five of a kind with tens.

Four of a kind is four dice of the same value with one other die. Four of a kind with kings will beat four of a kind with tens. Where the same four of a kind is thrown, the fifth die is taken into account: A, A, A, A, J would beat A, A, A, A, 10.

A high straight or big street is A, K, Q, J, 10.

A low straight or small street is K, Q, J, 10, 9.

Three of a kind is three dice of the same value with two other dice. Where the same three of a kind is thrown, the other dice are taken into account: K, K, K, Q, 10 beats K, K, K, J, 9.

Two pair is two sets of pairs and any other dice. For example, Q, Q, J, J, 9. The value of the highest pair counts against other two pairs: K, K, 9, 9, J would beat J, J, 10, 10, A.

Where the two pair is the same, the value of the fifth die is taken into account: Q, Q, J, J, 10 would beat Q, Q, J, J, 9.

One pair is two dice of the same value. For example A, A, K, J, 9. Where the two dice are of the same value, the highest other die is taken into account: A, A, Q, 10, 9 would beat A, A, J, 10, 9. Where the pair are the same value and the highest other die is matched, the value of the next highest die is taken into account and so on: Q, Q, K, J, 9 would beat Q, Q, K,10, 9; A, A, K, Q, J would beat A, A, K, Q, 9.

A tied hand does not count as the next player must have a throw that is higher than the previously announced hand. A player can announce a hand that is lower than he actually passes on. For example, a player can announce a pair when he actually has three of a kind. This strategy is sometimes used to ambush a player who is doing well and has not yet lost.

There may be four of a kind in the first throw. This may be passed to the next player as a small street. The player removes one die and throws it. The following player assumes that the player is aiming to get a big street. If he throws a king, queen, jack, 10 or 9, then the player will assume that he has failed to get the big street. The player refuses to accept the throw, removes the hat and then finds that there is a four of a kind which is higher than a big street.

> **Example**
>
> Player A throws 9, 9, 9, 9, K and announces a small street.
>
> Player B removes the king and leaves the four nines under that hat. He throws the dice he removed on the table and gets a jack. The hand is now 9, 9, 9, 9, J. He announces a big street.
>
> Player C does not accept and removes the hat.
>
> Player C loses as four of a kind ranks higher than a big street.
>
> If a player throws the maximum ranking throw of five aces, this is usually revealed instantly as the person who throws this hand cannot be beaten. The following player is then treated as a loser. The next game starts from the loser.

Playing the game

Each player throws a die, the one with the highest score goes first. The player puts all the dice under the hat and shakes them. He announces his hand and passes the dice to the player sitting on either his left or right.

The game then continues in the direction selected (clockwise or anti-clockwise). The next player has the option of either accepting the throw or refusing it. If he refuses it, he removes the hat revealing the dice to all the other players. If the throw is equal to or more than that announced, the second player loses and is given a card. If the throw is less than that announced, the first player loses and is given a card. The game then recommences with the losing player starting again.

If the player accepts the throw, he must pass on a higher ranking throw to the next player. To get a higher ranking hand he is allowed to shake either all or some of the dice.

Dice may be removed from the hat and the remaining dice shaken or dice may be left under the hat and some removed and thrown on the table. Players must always pass on a higher ranking hand. Even if you do not have a higher ranking hand, you can bluff.

With each new game the direction of play can be changed, as the first player decides whether to go clockwise or anti-clockwise. Once all the cards have been distributed, the direction of play can no longer be changed.

figure 15.3 example of poker dice game

Figure 15.3 shows the throws made by three players – A, B and C.

Player A goes first. He shakes all the dice, looks at what he has thrown and announces two jacks and passes the hat to the next player.

Player B accepts the throw and looks at the dice. He removes the jacks from the hat and places them on the table. He then shakes the remaining dice and looks at them. He announces two jacks, two tens and a 9.

Player C removes the two tens from the hat and places them on the table. There are now two jacks and two tens on the table. The remaining die is left under the hat and shaken in an attempt to get a full house. Although he fails to get a full house he has managed to beat B's throw as the ace is higher than a nine. He announces two jacks, two tens and an ace.

Player A accepts this and also attempts to get a full house by shaking the one remaining die in the hat. He throws a jack and gets a full house. He announces three jacks and two tens or a full house jacks over tens.

Player B accepts. He removes the third jack from the hat and places it on the table. He puts the two tens under the hat and shakes the dice. To beat the full house of jacks over tens he needs to throw two queens, two kings, two aces or another jack. He actually throws a king and a 9. This is not enough to beat the previous score so he lies and announces a full house with three jacks and two queens.

Player C refuses to accept the throw and removes the hat. The bluff is revealed and player B loses.

Player B receives a card and the game begins again from player B.

Keeping score

Cards are usually used to keep the score. As the game is often played in pubs, beer mats are used. A player who loses a game receives a card. When all the cards have been used, players then return them when they win. The object of the game is to end up with no cards. Players with no cards drop out of the game. The last remaining player is the loser. If playing for drinks, he pays for the next round.

Number of cards used

Players will usually agree between themselves how many cards
will be used. As a rough guide, for two to three players, six
cards should be used and for four to six players, eight cards
should be used.

16

video poker machines

In this chapter you will learn:
- how to play video poker
- about payout odds
- about playing tips.

What is video poker?

Video poker is a game based on five-card draw. It is played on a machine, which displays the cards dealt much like a computer game. The player bets against the machine, which acts as the dealer and the banker. The object of the game is to make the highest ranking poker hand possible. Video poker differs from most other slot machines because the skill of the player affects the outcome of the game.

A winning hand is paid a fixed return. The payouts for winning hands are displayed on the machine. The higher the ranking of the hand the greater the returns. The payouts vary depending on where the game is played in accordance with local legislation on gaming returns.

Video poker differs from a traditional game of five-card draw in a number of ways:

- There in only one player so it is not necessary to beat other players' hands.
- It is a much faster game.
- The payout odds for particular hands are fixed.
- It does not involve bluffing.

Types of machine

There are a number of different types of machine with slight variations in the rules. The most popular games are jacks or better, deuces wild and joker wild. Games can also be played where three hands at a time are played. For beginners, jacks or better is a simpler game to play. The returns for a royal flush on some machines are fixed, on others there is a progressive jackpot that accumulates each time a game is played. Machines with a fixed payout are called flat tops.

How to play

The aim is to make the highest ranking poker hand possible that is in the payout schedule displayed on the machine. The minimum hand needed to win varies with different games.

The player inserts sufficient coins or a smart card to play. Smart cards are like credit cards that can be purchased and charged up with money at the cashpoint. Minimum stakes are often in multiples of five coins. If you decide to play with fewer than five coins, you will need to press the deal button. If you insert all five coins, the machine will automatically deal a five-card hand.

A standard deck of 52 cards is randomly shuffled and dealt as in a normal game of poker. The player receives a five-card hand. The player then has the opportunity to improve the hand by discarding cards and being dealt new ones.

The player decides which cards to keep and presses the corresponding hold button. A hold can be cancelled by pressing the button a second time. The player may keep all the cards or discard any number of cards. It is possible to be dealt a winning hand with the initial five cards. This is usually indicated by a beep or a flashing light. When the player has decided which cards to keep, the draw/deal button is pressed. The machine will deal new cards to the hand. If a hand wins, it will be paid out according to the payout schedule displayed on the machine.

Ranking of hands

Hands are ranked in the same way as five-card draw (see page 23). For games where there are wildcards, there are additional hands that include the wildcard, such as five of a kind. A royal flush made with a wildcard is considered a lower ranking hand than a regular royal flush.

Payout odds for different games

The odds given here are intended only as a guide and will vary depending on where the game is played.

Jacks or better

Jacks or better is the most popular game. To win you need to get a pair of jacks or better. The minimum stake is five coins.

Payout schedule

Hand	Payout per coin
Royal flush	250–800 or progressive jackpot
Straight flush	50
Four of a kind	25
Full house	6–9
Flush	5–6
Straight	4
Three of a kind	3
Two pair	2
Pair of jacks or better	1

Deuces wild

With deuces wild games, all twos are wildcards. This means that when you get a two you can use it to represent any card. If, for example, you have three aces and a two, the hand held will be four aces. Because there is a greater chance of getting a ranking hand, only hands of three of a kind or better win.

Payout schedule

Hand	Payout per coin
Royal flush	varies
Four deuces	200
Royal flush with deuces	25
Five of a kind	15
Straight flush	9
Four of a kind	5
Full house	3
Flush	2
Straight	2
Three of a kind	1

Joker wild

In the game of joker wild, an additional card of a joker is added to the deck making 53 cards. The joker is a wildcard. The additional joker makes it easier to achieve higher ranking hands, which is reflected in lower payout odds than jacks or better. You also need to get a higher hand to win. You need at least two pair or better to win.

Payout schedule

Hand	Payout per coin
Royal flush	varies
Five of a kind	100
Royal flush with joker	50
Straight flush	50
Four of a kind	20
Full house	8
Flush	7
Straight	5
Three of a kind	2
Two pair	1

Playing tips

Compare the payout schedules on each machine and select the best. Progressive machines offer the best value because they give you the opportunity to win a larger jackpot than flat top machines.

The overall return that a machine gives is usually expressed as a percentage. On some machines it is possible to get a return of over 100 per cent if they are played over a long term. Look for a machine that has already accumulated a large jackpot. In order to win the jackpot, around 45 hours of fast play is required. This requires a bankroll of several thousand coins. If a large jackpot has already accumulated, it will be possible to win it in a shorter time.

Always play the maximum possible stake as a smaller bet pays out lower odds. The maximum possible bet it usually five coins.

A jackpot with five coins inserted pays on average 4000 coins. With only one coin inserted it pays around 250.

Learn the playing strategy for video poker. This differs from traditional five-card draw because with video poker there is no bluffing involved. Strategies such as keeping a kicker to a pair are not correct for video poker.

Master jacks or better before graduating to other games. Jacks or better is the simplest game to learn.

Make sure the strategy you use is the correct one for the game you are playing. Games with wildcards like deuces and joker wild are more complex and require a different strategy from jacks or better.

Play slowly and carefully while you are learning. Hands like straights are not always immediately obvious, as the cards will rarely be displayed in the correct ascending or descending order. Don't forget that in a straight an ace can be used as a high or a low card.

Basic strategy for jacks or better

The following gives a simple strategy for jacks or better that is suitable for beginners.

1   Hold any hand of a straight or over in the ranking.
2   If four cards to a royal flush are held draw one (including to a winning flush).
3   Four cards to a straight flush or a flush – draw one.
4   Three of a kind – draw two.
5   Two pair – draw one.
6   Pair – draw three.
7   Three-card royal flush – draw two.
8   Four-card straight – draw one.
9   Three-card straight flush – draw two.
10 Two high cards J, Q, K, A – draw three.
11 Three high cards (jack and over) – hold two of the same suit. If different suits, hold the two lowest high cards.
12 Four-card straight – draw one.
13 High card – draw four.
14 Nothing – draw five.

Deuces wild strategy

The strategy depends on how many deuces are held.

Four deuces: draw no cards.

Three deuces: if no royal flush or five of a kind – draw two.

Two deuces: with four of a kind or better do not draw; with four cards to a royal flush – draw one; other hands – hold the deuces and draw three.

No deuces: hold any royal flush, straight or flush.

Four cards to a royal straight, straight or flush – draw one.

Four of a kind – draw one.

Three of a kind – draw two.

One pair – draw three.

Three cards to a straight flush – draw two.

Same-suited high cards 10, J, Q, K – hold two.

Nothing – draw five.

Kings or better joker wild strategy

The strategy depends on whether or not you hold a joker.

Joker held

Hold hands that are three of a kind or higher.

Hold four cards to a royal flush.

Hold any four-card straight flush and a four-card flush if it includes K or A or both.

Hold three cards to a royal flush

Hold a paying pair of high cards (king, ace).

Hold any three cards to a straight flush.

Hold any four-card flush without king or ace.

Hold consecutive four-card straights

If none of these – hold the joker.

No joker held

Hold all paying hands.

Hold a four-card royal flush.

Hold any four cards to a straight flush and any three cards to a royal flush.

Hold four cards to any flush.

Hold any pair of twos to queens.

Hold any three cards to a straight flush.

Hold any four-card consecutive straight.

Hold two cards to a royal flush if one of the cards is a ace or king.

Hold unsuited king and ace.

Hold king or ace alone.

Hold two suited royal flush cards lower than king or ace.

If none of these – draw five.

glossary

ante a bet made before any cards have been dealt

babies low-value cards

bicycle see wheel

big blind a bet on the first round of betting in Texas hold 'em

blind bet a bet made without looking at your cards

bluff tricking the other players into thinking that you have a really good hand

board the community cards in games such as hold 'em and Omaha

bone another name for a chip

bug a joker

bullet an ace

burnt card a card that is removed from the deck and not used in play. Often several of the top cards will be removed before hands are dealt to combat cheating by the dealer

button a plastic marker used in casino games to denote an imaginary dealer to ensure that no player gains an advantage from his position relative to the actual dealer

by me a verbal statement in draw poker that a player is not exchanging any cards

call a verbal statement that a player will match the previous bet

calling station a player who hardly ever raises

chip a plastic disc used in place of money for betting

commission a charge made by the casino for the use of its facilities

community cards cards that can be used by all the players to make up their best five-card poker hand in games such as hold 'em and Omaha

dead man's hand two pair of aces over eights

deuce two

door card in stud poker the first card that is dealt face up

draw exchanging cards in your hand for cards from the deck

fives five cards of the same value – this hand is only possible where wildcards are used

flat tops video poker machines with fixed payout odds

flop the deal where the first three community cards are revealed in hold 'em

flush five cards of the same suit

fold withdraw from the game

freak a wildcard

full house three cards of the same value with a pair, for example, three aces and two sixes

hole cards a player's cards that are dealt face down

house advantage an adjustment made to the odds on banking games that allows the casino to make a profit

kicker in draw poker this is a card retained to make it more difficult for your opponents to guess your hand

knave a jack

knock in draw poker a player may knock on the table to signify that no cards are required

limit the maximum bet

low poker a game where players aim to have the lowest ranking poker hand

marked cards cards that have been marked in some way so that a cheat can identify their values from looking at their backs

monster a high-ranking hand

muck pile the pile of cards from players who have folded

nuts having a hand in games such as hold 'em and Omaha that is the best possible hand, one that cannot be beaten by any other player

odds a ratio expressing your chances of losing against your chances of winning, for example, odds of 2/1 means you have two chances of losing against one chance of winning

open to place the first bet

openers cards needed to open a pot, for example, two jacks are needed to open a jackpot. In some games, a minimum hand is needed before an opening bet can be made. In a jackpot, two jacks are needed, for a queen pot – two queens, etc.

over used as a short way of expressing two pair, for example, queens over tens means two queens and two tens

paint any court card, for example, king, queen or jack

pig a high and low hand

pocket card cards that are dealt face down

poker face having complete control over your facial expressions so that you do not give your opponents any clues about your hand

pokies video poker machines

progressives video poker machines with increasing jackpots

rake a charge made by the casino for the use of its facilities, usually a percentage of the pot

river the last round of betting

rock a player who always folds unless he has a really good hand

run another name for a straight

runt a hand lower than a pair

school a group of players who regularly play together

see has the same meaning as 'call'

set three cards of the same value

showdown when the players reveal their hands

sitting pat a player who takes no cards in draw poker

stake the amount of money bet

straddle a method of betting where the previous bet is doubled – the doubling of previous bets usually continues for a predetermined number of times

straight five cards of any suit in consecutive order

street a round of betting – first street is the first round of betting, second street the second and so on

stud a form of poker where some cards are dealt face up

sweeten to add money to the pot, usually in the form of an ante-bet

technician someone who is skilled at manipulating the cards so that he can deal himself a good hand

threes three cards of the same value

trey a three

trips three cards of the same value

wheel 5, 4, 3, 2, A in low poker

wildcard a nominated card that can be used in place of any other card to form a poker hand

taking it further

Gamblers' help organizations

Great Britain

GamCare
2 & 3 Baden Place
Crosby Row
London
SE1 1YW
Tel 020 7378 5200
Fax 020 7378 5237
Helpline 0845 6000 133 (24 hour, 7 days a week.)
Email info@gamcare.org.uk
www.gamcare.org.uk/

United States

Gamblers Intergroup
PO Box 7
New York
New York 10116
Tel 212 903 4400

Australia

Gamblers' Anonymous
PO Box 142
Burwood
NSW 1805
Tel (02) 9564 1574
www.gamblersanonymous.org.au/

Regulatory bodies and arbitration services

The Gambling Commission
www.gamblingcommission.org.uk/

Interactive Gaming Council Canada
175–2906 West Broadway
Vancouver
BC V6K 2G8
Canada
Tel 604 732 3833
Fax 604 732 3866
www.igcouncil.org/contact.php

Independent Betting Arbitration Service (IBAS)
PO Box 4011
London
E14 5BB
www.ibas-uk.com/

Online poker rooms

PartyPoker
Licenced and regulated by the government of Gibraltar
www.partypoker.com/

Ladbrokespoker.com
Operated by the world's biggest betting and gaming company. It
is licensed in Gibraltar and regulated by British gaming rules. Its
card-shuffling procedure is audited
www.ladbrokespoker.com/

Paradise Poker
Located in San José, Costa Rica
Its card-shuffling procedure is audited
www.paradisepoker.com/

The Gaming Club
Licensed by the government of Gibraltar
www.gamingclubpoker.com/

Poker Stars.com
Located in San José, Costa Rica.
Its card-shuffling procedure is audited
www.pokerstars.com/

aggressive players **16, 65, 153, 154**
alcohol **18, 120, 152**
all-in rule
    and internet poker **138, 141**
    and tournaments **147**
American Civil War **4**
ante-bets **20, 43, 116**
    five-card draw **77, 78**
    stud games **78, 79, 80, 86, 87**
    three-card poker **90**
anxiety **61**
Aussie Millions **151**
Australia
    casinos **123**
    law on internet poker **133**

banking games **128**
    and the law **115**
    see also Caribbean stud poker; pai
        gow poker
basic game **19–31**
    betting **20–1**
    number of players **20**
    variations **22**
    see also ranking of hands
betting **20–1, 42–51**
    blind bets **20, 43, 82, 85**
    and bluffing **46, 53, 63**
    call **44**
    Caribbean stud poker **86–7**
    in casinos **47,128**
    and cheatingv68, **73**
    five-card draw **77, 78**
    five-card stud **78–9**
    freeze out **50**
    limits for **44**
    Omaha **85**
    and pot odds **39**
    private games **20, 47–8, 116, 117**
    raising **44, 45–6**
    repetitive patterns of **63, 94**

running out of money **50–1**
    seven-card stud **45–6, 80, 81, 82**
    straddle method **48–9**
    strategy **45–6**
    table etiquette **118**
    Texas hold'em **82, 83**
        no-limit **49–50**
    time taken to bet **63**
    in turn **118**
    using a set limit **47–8**
    see also ante-bets; folding
Binion, Benny **5, 6**
blind bets **20, 43, 82, 85**
bluffing **46, 52–8**
    and body language **63–4**
    five-card draw **53, 57, 94–5, 97–8**
    how often to bluff **57–8**
    and lying **60–1**
    semi-bluffing **53**
    spotting in other players **58**
    Texas hold'em **53, 55, 56–7, 64, 65**
    and tournament play **54, 153, 154**
    what it is **53**
    when to bluff **53–7**
body language **15, 58, 59–65, 120**
    assessing the competition **64, 153**
    bluffing and lying **60–1**
    controlling **63–4**
    and internet poker **65, 142**
    tells **60, 61–3, 64, 65, 120**
    and type of player **65**
brag **2**
Britain see United Kingdom
Brunson, Doyle 'Texas Dolly' **6**
burning cards **73, 75**
    in internet poker **136**

cameras
    in casinos **74**
    cheating using **72**
Canadian casinos **123**

cards
  burning **73, 75**
  cold decks **72**
  combating cheating **72–5**
  cutting **70–1, 73**
  dealing extra cards **69–70**
  holding **67**
  keeping in view **117**
  looking at **62–3**
  marked **68–9, 73, 118**
  and private games **119**
  revealing **118–19**
  shuffling and dealing **74–5**
    in casinos **129**
  touching another player's **119**
Caribbean stud poker **5, 6, 86–7, 115, 124**
  betting **86–7, 109**
  house advantage **12, 108**
  online **5**
  payout odds **87**
  strategy **108–9**
cash, bets made with **20**
casinos **121–30**
  betting in **47, 128**
  British **122, 125**
  card room etiquette **127–8**
  and Caribbean stud poker **86–7, 124, 128**
  cheats in **72, 124–5**
  chips **20, 124, 126, 127**
  commission **12**
  comp schemes **126, 129, 130**
  compared with private games **113, 114, 124**
  Continental European **122, 125**
  costs of gambling in **11–12, 125**
  entry requirements **126**
  and fair play **67, 73–4, 124–5, 128–9**
  games played in **124**
  and gaming laws **122**
  high rollers (whales) **130**
  house advantage **12**
  online **132**
  organization of play **127**
  and pai gow poker **88–90**
  records of players **129**
  rules **12–13, 123**
  selecting a casino **123**
  self-exclusion schemes **18**
  southern hemisphere **123**
  stakes **126–7**
  subliminal practices **126**
  three-card poker **90–1**
  tipping **125**
  and tournaments **122, 142, 144**
  US and Canada **123, 125**
charity, playing poker for **115**

cheating **66–75**
  betting light **68**
  by dealers **69–71, 73, 74–5**
  casinos and fair play **67, 73–4, 124–5**
  cold decks **72**
  collusion **71–2**
  combating **72–5, 113–14, 119**
  false calling of a hand **72**
  holding cards **67**
  and internet poker **134–5, 140**
  marked cards **68–9, 73, 73–4, 118**
  and private games **67, 113–14, 118, 119, 120**
  reflective surfaces **67**
  stealing chips **71**
  use of modern technology **72**
checking **20, 43, 55, 65**
chips **20**
  betting using a set limit **47–8**
  casino chips **20, 124, 126, 127, 128**
    running out of **127**
  clear handling of **118**
  exchanging money for **9–10**
  palming **68**
  players running short of **56**
  and private games **119**
  stealing **71**
  touching another player's **119**
  and tournaments **147, 153, 154**
clearing hands **73**
clubs, private members' **115**
cold decks **72**
collusion **71–2, 125**
  and internet poker **134–5, 140**
commission, casino gambling **12**
community cards **22**
  let it ride poker **92**
  Omaha **85, 107**
  Texas hold'em **82–3, 84, 104, 105, 106, 107**
competition, assessing **64**
Continental European casinos **122, 125**
costs of gambling **10–12**
  in casinos **125**
  tournaments **146**
Crowell, Joseph **3**
Crown Australian Poker Championship **151**
cutting the cards **70–1, 73**

Dandolos, Nick 'the Greek' **6–7**
dealers **20**
  in casinos **74, 124–5, 127**
    Caribbean stud poker **86–7, 108–9**
    pai gow poker **88–90**
    and tournaments **147**
  cheating by **69–71**
    combating **73**

cutting the cards **70–1**
dealing extra cards **69–70**
shuffling and dealing **74–5**
in internet poker **136**
let it ride poker **92**
dealing cards **74–5**
deuces wild **165, 168**
dice games **3**
see also poker dice
discarded cards
combating cheating **75**
five-card draw **77, 78, 95–6, 97**
muck pile **20, 44, 67, 70**
disputes
and casinos **125**
with internet poker sites **141–2**
and private games **113, 120**
and tournaments **147**
draw poker **4, 10, 22, 126**
odds **33, 34–7, 95**
see also five–card draw

etiquette
card rooms **127–8**
private games **117–19**
European Championship **151**
extra cards, dealing **69–70**

facial expressions **62**
fair play, ensuring **63–4, 67, 73–4, 124–5, 128–9**
false calling of a hand **72**
famous poker players **6–7**
five-card draw **77–8, 115, 124**
betting **77, 78**
bluffing **53, 57, 94–5, 97–8**
cheating with extra cards **70**
discarded cards **77, 78, 95–6, 97**
holding a pair **97–8**
practising **14**
ranking of hands **77, 94–5**
strategy **94–8**
and video poker **163**
what hand to play **94**
five-card stud **5, 34, 78–9, 115**
betting **78–9**
practising **14**
ranking of hands **78–9, 98–101**
strategy **98–101**
suits **78**
folding **20, 21, 36, 44, 102**
and bluffing **46, 53, 54, 55, 56, 57–8**
and internet poker **135, 136**
knowing when to fold **46–7**
looking at cards after **63**
in turn **117–18**
freeze out **50**
freeze out/no re-buy tournaments **145**

GamCare certification **141–2**
glasses, acting as mirrors **67**
Green, Jonathan H., *An Exposure of the Arts and Miseries of Gambling* **3**

hand rankings *see* ranking of hands
Hickok, 'Wild Bill' **7**
high card **92**
hole cards **45, 80, 85**
Holliday, Doc **4**
hosting private games **119–20**
house advantage **12, 108**
Hoyles' Games **3, 4**

Interactive Gaming Council (IGC) **141**
internet poker **5, 131–42**
advantages of **134**
all-in abuse **141**
body language **65**
card rooms **132**
casinos **132**
chatting to other players **139**
cheating **134–5, 140**
cost of playing **11**
depositing and withdrawing money **137**
disconnections **138**
disputes **141–2**
fairness of **134**
history of **132–3**
how it works **135–8**
joining a game **138**
and the law **133, 134, 136**
passwords **137, 140, 141**
phishing **141**
playing safe **139–40**
rake **132**
registration **136–7**
software **134, 137**
speed of **10**
strategy **142**
tournaments **144, 149**

Jack Binion World Open **150**
jacks or better **164–5, 167**
joker wild **166, 167, 168–9**

kings or better **168–9**

Ladbrokes Poker Million Tournament **141**
Las Vegas **5, 6, 150**
the law
and internet poker **133, 134, 136**
and private games **114–15**
let it ride poker **92, 111**
liar's dice (poker dice) **6, 155–61**

Lillard, John, *Poker Stories* **13**
lollapalooza **13**
low poker **24–5**
lying **60–1, 63**

marked cards **68–9, 73–4, 118**
mirrors **67**
money management **9, 10–12**
  internet poker **137**
Moss, Johnny **7**
muck pile **20, 44, 67, 70**

nas **2**
New Orleans **2, 3**
New Zealand casinos **123**
no-limit games **49–50, 54**
novice players **65**
nuts
  Omaha **108**
  Texas hold'em **105–7**

odds **32–41**
  of being dealt a particular hand
    33–4
  Caribbean stud poker **87**
  draw games **33, 34–7, 95**
  high card **92**
  and house advantage **12**
  let it ride poker **92**
  pai gow poker **89**
  pair plus **90, 91**
  pot odds **39**
  stud games **37–9**
  three-card poker **91**
  video poker **163–6**
  wildcards **33, 40–1**
Omaha **6, 85–6, 115**
  betting **85**
  bluffing **53**
  in casinos **124, 126, 127**
  community cards **85, 107**
  cost of playing **10, 11**
  flop **85, 107**
  hole cards **85, 107**
  nuts **108**
  odds **37**
  online **11**
  practising **14**
  ranking of hands **85–6**
  strategy **107–8**
online poker *see* internet poker
origins of poker **2–3**

pai gow poker **88–90, 115, 124**
  house advantage **12**
  odds **89**
  ranking of hands **88, 109–11**
  strategy **109–111**

pair plus **90, 91**
palming chips **68**
Party Poker **132**
PartyPoker.com Million **151**
phishing **141**
player profiles **16**
playing strategies **93–111**
  Caribbean stud poker **108–9**
  five-card draw **94–8**
  five-card stud **98–101**
  internet poker **142**
  let it ride poker **111**
  Omaha **107–8**
  pai gow poker **109–111**
  private games **120**
  seven-card stud **101–3**
  Texas hold'em **103–7**
  video poker **166–9**
playing tips **8–18**
  appreciating chances of winning
    16–17
  costs of gambling **9, 10–12**
  exchanging money for chips **9–10**
  finding your game **12–15**
  knowing when to stop **17–18**
  player profiles **16**
  record-keeping **15–16**
  tournaments **152–3**
  varying your play **17**
Pochen **2**
poker dice **6, 155–61**
  keeping score **160**
  number of cards used **161**
  playing the game **158–60**
  ranking of dice **157–8**
Poker Hall of Fame **6–7**
poque **2**
pot limit games **50**
pot limit/no pot limit tournaments **146**
pot odds **39**
pots
  in casinos **127, 128**
  combating cheating **73**
  increasing the pot **20**
  main pot and side pots **50–1**
  size of and bluffing **54**
  split pots in Texas hold'em **83**
  stealing chips from the pot **71**
  and table etiquette **118**
practising poker **13–14, 152**
primero **2**
private games
  advantages of **113**
  betting **20, 47, 116, 117**
  breaks during **118, 120**
  cheating at **67, 118, 119**
    combating **72–3, 113–14, 119,
      120**

compared with casinos **113, 114, 124**
cost of playing **10, 11**
deciding the rules **116–17**
disadvantages of **113–14**
disputes **113**
and five-card draw **94**
hosting **119–20**
knowing when to stop **17**
and the law **114–15**
learning poker through **113**
quitting playing **114**
ranking of hands **29, 30**
refreshments **120**
rules of **13**
strategy **120**
table etiquette **117–19**
and tournaments **152**
understanding the odds **33**
wildcards in **40–1, 116, 120**
private games **ix, 5, 112–20**
private members' clubs **115**
prizes at tournaments **147–8**
problem gambling **18**
progressive poker **90–1**
progressive stack re-buy tournaments **145**

ranking of hands **13, 20, 21**
and betting strategy **46**
blaze **26, 27**
and bluffing **56**
bobtail straight **27**
cards speak rule **31**
cats and dogs **28–9**
Dutch/skip straight or kilter **26, 27**
five and dime **29**
five of a kind **29–30, 41**
five-card draw **77, 94–8**
five-card stud **78–9, 98–101**
flush **23, 24, 26, 36–7**
in Omaha **107**
in pai gow poker **110**
in Texas hold'em **104**
four flush **27**
four of a kind **23, 24, 36**
full house **21, 23, 24**
in draw games **36, 97, 98**
in Omaha **85, 86**
in pai gow poker **110–11**
and wildcards **41**
let it ride poker **92**
low poker **24–5**
no pair, highest card **23**
odds of being dealt a particular hand **33–4**
Omaha **85–6, 107–8**
one pair **21, 23, 24, 97, 99, 109**

pai gow poker **88, 109–11**
and private games **116**
recognizing and practising **13–14**
round the corner straight **29**
royal flush **22, 23, 29, 33**
in Texas hold'em **106**
in video poker **163**
and wildcards **41**
seven-card stud **80, 81, 82, 101–3**
showdowns **21, 24, 31, 72**
skeet/pelter/bracket **26, 27**
standard **22–4**
straight **21, 23, 24, 26**
pai gow poker **110**
in seven-card stud **101, 102**
in Texas hold'em **104**
straight flush **21, 22, 23, 99–100, 110**
suits **30**
Texas hold'em **104–7**
three of a kind (trips) **21, 23, 24, 30, 35–6, 98**
pai gow poker **109–10**
in seven-card stud **101, 102, 103**
and wildcards **41**
three-card poker **90, 91**
two pair **21, 23, 24, 85, 86, 109–10**
video poker **163, 164, 165, 166**
wildcards **29–30, 40–1**
re-buy tournaments **145**
record-keeping **15–16**
reflective surfaces **67**
rules
casinos **12–13, 123**
private games **13**

safety, and internet poker **139–40**
satellite tournaments **148, 150**
Schenk poker **4**
semi-bluffing **53**
seven-card stud **5, 80–2, 115, 124**
betting **45–6, 80, 81, 82**
bluffing **53**
in casinos **126, 127**
cost of playing **10**
door cards **80**
folding **102**
hole cards **45, 80**
odds **37**
practising **14**
ranking of hands **80, 81, 82, 101–3**
showdown **102**
strategy **101–3**
showdowns **21, 24, 31, 72**
seven-card stud **102**
Texas hold'em **83**
shuffling cards **74–5**
smart cards, and video poker **163–4**

speed tournaments **150**
stakes **126–7**
    calculating stake level **11**
    video poker **166–7**
straddle method of betting **48–9**
strangers, playing with **64, 72,
    113–14, 153**
strategy
    betting **45–6**
    see also playing strategies
strong, experienced players **65**
suits, ranking of **30, 78, 80**

tables
    avoiding reflective surfaces **67**
    table etiquette at private games
    117–19
tali **3**
technicians **69–70, 73**
televized poker **57**
tells **60, 61–3, 64, 65, 120**
    acting **62**
    anxiety **61**
    betting patterns **63**
    looking at cards **62–3**
    stance **62**
Texas hold'em **5, 6, 82–4, 115**
    betting **82, 83**
        no-limit **49–50**
    bluffing **53, 55, 56–7, 64, 65**
    in casinos **124, 126, 127**
    community cards **82–3, 84, 104,
        105, 106, 107**
    cost of playing **10**
    the deal **82–3**
    fixed limit **44**
    flop **56, 57, 82–3**
        looking at cards after **62**
        strategy before and after **104–5**
    no-limit **49–50, 54**
    nuts **105–7**
    odds **37, 38–9, 40**
    and Omaha **85**
    online **65**
    practising **14**
    on the river **65**
    semi-bluffing **53**
    showdown **83**
    split pots **83**
    strategy **103–7**
    on the turn **65**
three-card poker **90–1**
tipping, in casinos **125**
Tournament of Champions of Poker
    150
tournaments **122, 143–54**
    advantages of **144**
        bluffing **54, 153, 154**
        breaks **144, 152**
        costs **146**
        duration of **144**
        entry requirements **146**
        freeze out/no re-buy **145**
        internet poker **144, 149**
        major tournaments **150–1**
        organization of play **147**
        playing tips **152–3**
        pot limit/no pot limit **146**
        prizes **147–8**
        progressive stack re-buy **145**
        re-buy **145**
        satellites **148, 150**
        speed tournaments **150**
        UK competitions **148–9**

understanding the odds *see* odds
United Kingdom
    casinos **122, 125**
    tournaments **148–9**
    UK law
        and internet poker **133, 134**
        and private games **114–15**
United States of America **2, 3–5**
    casinos **123, 125, 129**
    law on internet poker **133**
    US law
        and private games **115**
        on taxation of winnings **154**

Victoria, Queen **4**
video poker **5, 6, 162–9**
    deuces wild **165, 168**
    jacks or better **164–5, 167**
    joker wild **166, 167, 168–9**
    payout odds **163–6**
    playing tips **166–7**
    ranking of hands **163, 164, 165,
        166**
    and smart cards **163–4**

wildcards **5, 13, 116, 120**
    ranking hands with **29–30**
    understanding the odds **33, 40–1**
winning, understanding your chances
    of **16–17**
women players **146**
World Heads-up Poker Championship
    151
World Series of Poker **5, 6, 144, 148,
    150**
    trial **151**